30

RESISTANCE TO
MULTICULTURALISM

RESISTANCE TO MULTICULTURALISM

ISSUES AND INTERVENTIONS

Jeffery Scott Mio
Gene I. Awakuni

BRUNNER/MAZEL
Taylor & Francis Group

Special Guest Authors

Lori Barker-Hackett

California State Polytechnic University, Pomona

Laurie A. Roades

California State Polytechnic University, Pomona

USA	Publishing Office:	BRUNNER/MAZEL *A member of the Taylor & Francis Group* 325 Chestnut Street Philadelphia, PA 19106 Tel: (215) 625-8900 Fax: (215) 625-2940
	Distribution Center:	BRUNNER/MAZEL *A member of the Taylor & Francis Group* 47 Runway Road, Suite G Levittown, PA 19057 Tel: (215) 269-0400 Fax: (215) 269-0363
UK		BRUNNER/MAZEL *A member of the Taylor & Francis Group* 11 New Fetter Lane London EC4P 4EE Tel: +44 171 583 0490 Fax: +44 171 583 0581

RESISTANCE TO MULTICULTURALISM: Issues and Interventions

1 2 3 4 5 6 7 8 9 0

Printed by Braun-Brumfield, Ann Arbor, MI, 1999.
Cover design by Claire C. O'Neill.

A CIP catalog record for this book is available from the British Library.
∞ The paper in this publication meets the requirements of the ANSI Standard Z39.48-1984 (Permanence of Paper).

Library of Congress Cataloging-in-Publication Data

Mio, Jeffery Scott.
    Resistance to multiculturalism: issues and interventions / Jeffery Scott Mio and Gene I. Awakuni.
      p. cm.
    Includes bibliographical references and index.

    1. Multiculturalism. 2. Multicultural education. 3. Mental health education. 4. Racism. 5. Stereotype (Psychology). 6. Avoidance (Psychology).
I. Awakuni, Gene I. II. Title.

HM1271.M56 1999
306.44'6—dc21

99-045387

ISBN 0-87630-954-6 (case: alk. paper)
ISBN 0-87630-955-4 (pa.: alk. paper)

To Dottie Morris and Kelly Wilson, my first Ph.D. students,
who were the driving forces behind me doing the right thing.
—JSM

To my wife, Diana, for her unwavering support;
and to my parents for sharing their incredible wisdom.
—GIA

CONTENTS

8

9

10

PREFACE

All behavior is learned and displayed in a cultural context. Thus, cultural context—whether acknowledged or not—becomes an important aspect of human behavior. It is incumbent upon all mental health professionals to understand the importance of culture and to apply meaningful interventions when working with clients.

Mental health training also occurs in a cultural context. Unfortunately, many, if not most, of those who are trained to provide services to individuals of all ethnic and cultural backgrounds have received their training from instructors who were trained to think of people as interchangeable parts. Consequently, ethnicity and culture are considered nuisance variables for which one must control or, even worse, elements that can be ignored. Moreover, mental health trainees are themselves, citizens in a cultural context. The broader society is awash with controversy over issues of race relations and the importance of ethnic and cultural variation in a country whose view of itself is that of a melting pot where everyone is eventually homogenized into a consistent soup. Subtle and not-so-subtle forms of racism have arisen in response to those who claim that ethnicity and culture matter.

This book is based on observations made during 10 years of teaching multiculturalism at the graduate and undergraduate levels. Over the years, I have been interested in the issues involved in how to teach this topic when the participants are resistant to multiculturalism or are in denial about their own naiveté. In the past, when most cross-cultural and multicultural courses were optional in graduate programs, only students who were interested in the topic enrolled in the courses. Although these courses were typically disappointingly low in enrollment, they were easier to teach, given the intrinsic motivation of the students. However, with the requirement by professional organizations that multicultural issues be covered in the graduate curricula of the helping professions, students who otherwise might have avoided the topic began taking the courses. These were exactly the students who needed to take the courses, but they were also the most resistant. To use highly intense methods of persuasion might result in a reactance, causing those who are resistant to hold onto their original beliefs much more strongly (classical reactance theory, or the "boomerang effect," Brehm & Brehm, 1981). To be overly subtle might not force these resistant individuals to experience the encounter that is so necessary to break down racism or resistance, as the racial identity literature suggests is important (Helms, 1990). In this book, I have compiled the techniques and interventions I have used or been exposed to and found effective in overcoming the resistance I have encountered. It is my most sincere hope that readers find at least some of these techniques to be useful in dealing with their own students.

Throughout this book, I have used the first person singular form. However, four chapters were cowritten with three of my colleagues. Dr. Gene I. Awakuni, the book's coauthor, is an administrator, and he and I have cowritten his chapters on overcoming resistance as he has seen it at the administrative level. Dr. Laurie A. Roades and I have coauthored a chapter on the use of allies in forming coalitions across demographic characteristics. This chapter is based on data we collected on clear allies when addressing not only multiculturalism but also sexism and heterosexism. Dr. Roades took the lead in writing this chapter, so her name appears as the senior author. Dr. Lori Barker-Hackett and I have coauthored a chapter about selected interventions beyond the classroom. She has had more experience than I in this area, and her insights into interventions at a broader level were invaluable. Hence, Dr. Barker-Hackett's name appears as the senior author of this chapter. In these four chapters, we have used the first-person plural form, "we."

In Chapter 1, I have tried to demonstrate that multiculturalism is scholarship of the highest order, as proposed by the highly respected Ernest Boyer of The Carnegie Foundation for the Advancement of Teaching (Boyer, 1987, 1990; Boyer & Hechinger, 1981). Thus, to oppose multiculturalism is to oppose scholarship itself.

In Chapters 2 and 3, I discuss modern forms of racism and resistance. Such forms are disguised as intellectual argument, founding principles, and other symbolic opposition to the multicultural movement. Many political initiatives are motivated by the desire to resist multiculturalism.

In Chapter 4, I discuss some cognitive forms of maintaining stereotypes, often called the "constructivist position." Here, stereotypes are not intentionally formed with malice, but they are formed out of normal cognitive processes. However, quite often, these stereotypes are maintained by media reinforcement.

Chapter 5 is the first chapter written with a coauthor. My colleague, Laurie Roades, and I have been collaborating on an investigation of what motivates people to form alliances across demographic divisions. Once such an alliance has been formed, what motivates these individuals to maintain their connection? Although we have just embarked on this journey, we have already collected some interesting information from individuals who are clearly allies of those of different ethnicity, sexual orientation, and gender.

In Chapter 6, I discuss the way in which I present standard multicultural information in my courses. Although the material is standard, I discuss the style in which I have presented the material, which seems to be effective in circumventing some resistance from some students. I also discuss my technique of assigning reaction papers, which help me to measure an individual's level of acceptance or rejection in a confidential manner. I am also able to give students feedback in personal and nonpublic ways. I use this technique because I feel that for many, these issues are difficult to discuss in an open manner without appearing to be racist. In public, we may adopt a socially acceptable manner of speaking about such issues, but we may privately hold quite different views. The reaction paper technique allows students to maintain their public stances while holding private conversations with me about these difficult issues. Finally, I discuss a game show, or debate, format that helps students to form connections with their colleagues concerning a particular ethnic minority group.

Chapter 7 is the second coauthored chapter. This one was written with my colleague Lori Barker-Hackett, who has had experience in working with large groups in nonacademic settings. Much of the material I present in Chapter 5 works well in a classroom, but it may not be appropriate in the setting of a large group where the multicultural specialist has only a limited amount of time to work with the participants. In Chapter 6, Dr. Barker-Hackett and I discuss those techniques that are transferable from the classroom to the situation of a single workshop and also those techniques specifically designed for the workshop setting.

Chapters 8 and 9 are the chapters I have coauthored with Gene I. Awakuni, who is currently the Vice President for Student Support Services (commonly known as "Student Affairs" on other campuses). Dr. Awakuni has held administrative positions at two other universities, and he has had experience in being the only (or nearly the only) administrator belonging to an ethnic minority group and of being one of many. Thus, he has seen resistance to multiculturalism in administrators when they felt the issue was being forced upon them by student or societal demands, and he has also seen resistance to multiculturalism by units, faculty, and students when it was the major initiative of the president of the university. Chapters 7 and 8 discuss these forms of resistance and strategies to address such resistance.

Finally, Chapter 10 is my attempt to examine the future of multiculturalism. The primary focus of the book is on resistance to ethnic minority diversity and on issues involving such diversity. However, "multiculturalism" is an inclusive term that comprises gender, sexual orientation, and physical ability, among other characteristics. Other individuals are much more qualified than I to discuss such elements in detail, but I have tried to identify the areas I see as being important in the coming years.

☐ References

Boyer, E. L. (1987). *College: The undergraduate experience in America*. New York: Harper & Row.

Boyer, E. L. (1990). *Scholarship reconsidered: Priorities of the professoriate*. Princeton, NJ: The Carnegie Foundation for the Advancement of Teaching.

Boyer, E. L., & Hechinger, F. M. (1981). *Higher learning in the nation's service*. Washington, DC: The Carnegie Foundation for the Advancement of Teaching.

Brehm, S., & Brehm, J. W. (1981). *Psychological reactance: A theory of freedom and control*. New York: Academic Press.

Helms, J. T. (1990). *Black and White racial identity: Theory, research, and practice*. New York: Greenwood.

ACKNOWLEDGMENTS

I would like to thank Sophia Aguirre and Laraine Turk for their contributions to this book, particularly in the chapters I coauthored with Dr. Awakuni. I would also like to thank current and former students in my courses on cross-cultural and multicultural issues. As you will see, many chapters are interspersed with comments and observations from some of these students, and their contributions are appreciated. I had indicated to my students that their comments might appear in my writings, so to preserve their anonymity, I list all of them, irrespective of whether their writings find expression in my work. The following are former students who deserve my thanks: Jim Adams, Yvette Alonso, Carolyn Ballard, Dan Banken, Robbin Barksdale, Dana Barnhart-Mendoza, Katherine Beigh, Natalie Bird, Leslie Bloom, Iva Brozicevic, Jan Cain, Susan Carmichael, Jamie Champion, John Chartier, Jason Davis, Andrea Dunn, Marian Flammang, Gina Formea, Lonn Friese, Bo-James Gilbert, Myron Goldberg, Victoria Gonzalez, Maria Gregoria, Nicole Hampson, Kathy Harris, Kelly Hazen, Chris Higginson, Loisee Hunter, Jay Iszo, John Johnson, Kristine Johnson, Susan Keortge, Christine Kim, Darrelle Koonce, Jenova Lacson, Ruth Lapsley, Lisanne Lara, Renee Mendoza, Kim Montag, Rebecca Munoz, Dottie Morris, Alejandrina Oceguera, Charlie Orsak, Gina Ortola, Christine Ota, Amita Patel, Cindy Ramirez, Jennifer Rogers, Louise Ryder, Jennifer Sanford, Donna Scott, Sonya Showalter, Bernadette Shupe, Eric Skansgaard, Marcia Staunton, Jennifer Steel, William Sze, Farhad Tamadon, Paul Tetu, Nancy Thomas, Carey Twitchell, Claudia Vasallo, Brian Vaughn, Janette West, Kelly Willson, Fumie Worthington, Gangaw Zaw, Sarah Zemke.

Jeffery Scott Mio

1

CHAPTER

Introduction

Imagine yourself in a faculty meeting in the late 1970s in which you propose that Multicultural Issues in Psychology be moved from the "minor" area of concentration to the "major" area on the list of potential topics for preliminary examinations. This seems like a reasonable request. Your Multicultural Psychology course is a required course in the program, every other required course's topic area is listed as a major area, many other nonrequired courses have topics that are listed as major areas, at least three of the student's four topic areas must be major areas, and it has been over 5 years since the American Psychological Association made a decision in its landmark Vail summit to require courses in multicultural issues to be included in graduate training programs (1973 National Conference on Levels and Patterns of Professional Training in Psychology, cited in Bernal & Padilla, 1982). Moreover, the Director of Clinical Training (DCT) is solidly behind this request and even encouraged you to make the proposal, with his backing. In the modern vernacular, this should be a "slam-dunk" decision. However, to your surprise, your colleagues vote the proposal down, even though you and your DCT have made both logical and passionate arguments in favor of the proposal.

Stunned, you and your DCT meet, wondering what happened. Weeks later, he suggests that you try to make this proposal again, giving your colleagues the benefit of the doubt by positing that perhaps they misunderstood your request. You state your case even more clearly and passionately than before, also emphasizing the APA's commitment to this area and its requirement that cross-cultural/multicultural content be infused into all graduate programs in psychology. This time, for sure, your colleagues will understand and pass the proposal. However, to your surprise, the response is even more heated than before. You hear comments like these: "Cross-cultural psychology is too limited an area to be considered a major topic area for prelims." "There is nothing to cross-cultural psychology." "We allowed it to be a required course—what more do you want?" "Cross-cultural psychology is unimportant." "Haven't we already dealt with this? No means no!"

At this point, you are probably thinking, "Well, in the late 1970s, even though it was 5 to 6 years after that Vail conference, the idea was probably still relatively new to those teaching in the profession. Moreover, most of those professors were 'old fogies' who were trained under an antiquated system, anyway, so of course they would be against new ideas." What would you say if I were to tell you that this happened to me in 1989? The surprising thing was that two of the most vocal opponents to moving Multicultural Issues from the minor list to the major list were relatively new and young professors, so even the old-fogies excuse cannot be applied. Also, what made this whole situation particularly amazing to me was that it was stimulated by a student's request. This student wanted to complete prelims in two areas, Hypnosis and Multicultural Issues, but because both of them were considered minor areas, he did not meet the criterion of choosing three major areas out of four. Disappointed, he dropped his pursuit of Multicultural Issues and selected a major area for study. Thus, the department not only let down the profession of psychology, it also let down one of its own students. Incidentally, it also convinced me that I should be looking elsewhere for employment, and even though I received tenure from the university later, I gave it up to leave such an environment.

Of course, this resistance to multicultural issues was not peculiar to my former department. As Bernal and Padilla (1982) concluded, the profession of psychology resisted the integration of cross-cultural issues into programs for nearly a decade after the injunction that programs should make this transition. They found that only about 20% of the accredited programs in psychology even had a course in cross-cultural psychology, and that none of them had required such a course for completion of the Ph.D. degree in their department. As I have stated in the past (Mio, 1989), this 20% figure was most likely an underestimate of the problem. Bernal and Padilla reported that 30 of the 106 accredited programs failed to respond to their survey, and one might speculate that these programs' nonparticipation was due to their lack of commitment to the area.

☐ Historical Efforts to Include Multiculturalism in Mental Health Training Programs

Sue et al. (1998) discuss many of the historical efforts to include multicultural issues in training programs in psychology and counseling. Because Derald Wing Sue was at the forefront of these efforts, his book does a much better job of discussing this history than I could do here. However, this book would be incomplete if I did not at least touch on the history of these efforts.

As indicated before, there was much institutional resistance to including multicultural issues in training programs. The Bernal and Padilla (1982) article documented the slow progress towards the integration of multicultural issues into curricula across the country. In 1986, when I arrived in the Department of Psychology of Washington State University—a department whose program had had APA accreditation status for nearly 30 years—no such course existed. The DCT of that institution knew the importance of this area, but there was no one to develop and teach a course in multicultural issues, so he asked me to develop such a course as soon as I arrived. Part of the motivation of the DCT was to "look good" for the APA accreditation site visit expected in a year or two, but I firmly believe that he was personally committed to the area as well. In speaking with colleagues across the country, I found that although programs had, in the past, not been disciplined for not having multicultural components, the accreditation site visitors were becoming more and more insistent in this area, and some programs were being placed on probation or given fewer than the maximum 5 years of accreditation for not taking the multicultural component seriously. Thus, the power structure of the organization was taking its own recommendations to heart, and the threat of deaccreditation was a powerful motivator that led programs to comply with the commitments of the profession. A lesson in this is that if one has a large enough stick, resistance can be overcome.

We arrived professionally at this point as a result of the efforts and consistent pressure of individuals such as James M. Jones (e.g., Jones, 1972), Derald Wing Sue (e.g., Sue, 1981), Stanley Sue (e.g., Sue, 1977), Martha E. Bernal (e.g., Bernal & Padilla, 1982), Robert V. Guthrie (e.g., Guthrie, 1976), and others too numerous to mention. Many others (e.g., Dalmas Taylor, Patrick Okura) also applied political pressure on the power structure of the APA.

The power structure of any organization is an important ally in effecting institutional change. As Sue et al. (1998) noted, it was Allen E. Ivey, President of Division 17 (the Division of Counseling Psychology) of the APA, who appointed Derald Wing Sue to head a committee to develop standard multicultural training competencies (Sue et al., 1982). Although this article was one of the most frequently cited in the multicultural arena (Ponterotto & Sabanini, 1989), the recommendations advocated in the article seemed to remain without institutional effect for nearly a decade. Sensing the need for rejuvenation of these recommendations, Thomas A. Parham, President of Division 17, again asked Derald Wing Sue to head a committee to update the past recommendations and state them more forcefully. This renewed effort resulted in another influential and often-cited article (Sue, Arredondo, & McDavis, 1992). However, sensing that these recommendations would be largely ignored or not interwoven into the fabric of the mental health profession, Derald Wing Sue (personal communication, September 1998) decided to take a proactive stance. He strove to get unanimity among important groups concerned with multicultural issues (e.g., The Association of Black Psychologists, The Asian American Psychological Association, The Hispanic Psychological Association, the Committee on Ethnic Minority Affairs, Division 17 of APA, Division 45 of APA) to endorse the Sue et al. (1998) multicultural competencies recommendations (which are based upon his past efforts) as standard practice in the mental health arena.

Sue et al. (1998) identified what they called "the seven deadly resistances" to integrating multiculturalism into training programs (p. 28). These resistances are presented sequentially; historically, when one resistance was addressed, another resistance took its place. Some of the resistances even contradicted earlier resistances, leaving one to question the motivations behind the resistances (see the box).

As is clear in the synopsis of the Sue et al. (1998) resistances and responses, many resistances (excuses) are raised to avoid integrating multicultural training competencies into mental health training programs, but none is legitimate (or at least, there are reasoned responses to demonstrate why these resistances are not valid).

☐ Scholarship Reconsidered

As most academicians are aware, one of the leading scholars in the United States was Ernest Boyer. Until his death in the early 1990s, he had dedicated much of his life examining the relationship between higher education and society. His books are legendary (e.g., Boyer, 1987, 1990; Boyer & Hechinger, 1981). His focus was on how society had an obligation to support colleges and universities. Because of this support, colleges and universities had a reciprocal obligation to society. Boyer and

The Seven Deadly Resistances and Responses to Them

Resistance	Response
1. Current theories of treatment are generalizable to all populations.	The sameness myth has been challenged by studies in areas such as worldviews, identity development, and individualism vs. collectivism. Time and time again, it has been found that issues of difference matter.
2. Conceptually sound multicultural standards do not exist.	At least since the time of the first multicultural competencies (Sue et. al., 1982), multicultural standards have existed.
3. The Sue et al. (1982) multicultural standards are too general.	Aside from the fact that mainstream counseling competencies are also vague and general, the Sue et al. (1982) competencies have been expanded and operationalized in the Sue et al. (1992) publication.
4. Multicultural competencies are too complex and detailed.	Quite clearly, this is contradictory to Resistance No. 3. However, culture is complex, just as therapy is complex, and good training will recognize these complexities.
5. It is difficult to measure the effectiveness of multicultural competency training.	Measuring therapy of any kind is difficult. However, in recent years, many multicultural assessment instruments have been developed (e.g., D'Andrea, Daniels, & Heck, 1991; LaFramboise, Coleman, & Hernandez, 1991; Ponterotto, Sanchez, & Magids, 1991; Sodowsky, Taffe, Gutkin, & Wise, 1992).
6. We need to wait until standards are developed for other groups, such as women, gays and lesbians, and the physically challenged.	Although there is some legitimacy to this argument, those who espouse it are merely attempting to delay implementation of an already developed set of standards.
7. Multiculturalism represents reverse racism and is anti-White.	Proponents of this view are merely taking cultural extremist positions and characterizing multicultural proponents as holding these extremist positions. It is not only unfair, but it is intellectually dishonest.

From Sue et al. (1998).

Hechinger (1981) discussed ways in which colleges have helped to solve the country's problems; for example, polytechnical schools helped to train individuals to build railroads and bridges in the 1800s, college and university researchers helped to solve military and medical problems that occurred on the battlefields during World War II, and colleges and universities have not only been testing grounds for racial integration, but have also produced professors and researchers who addressed racism in the 1960s and 1970s through their teachings and studies. The relationship between society and higher education is a constantly changing one as societal needs become higher education's charges. Boyer and Hechinger conclude:

> The center holds because the search for truth leads to the discovery of larger meanings that can be applied with integrity to life's decisions. This, we conclude, is higher learning's most essential mission in the nation's service. (p. 62)

In one of Boyer's last writings (Boyer, 1990), he examined what it meant to be a professor in today's higher educational system. Historically, he divided the American college system into three phases. In phase one, moral development was stressed. Professors were hired for their religious commitment, not their scholarly ability. In phase two, service became important, as the country had to have roads, bridges, and railroads built (as discussed in Boyer & Hechinger, 1981). In phase three, basic research was stressed. It had been present since the beginning of the American college and university movement, but it did not take hold until late in the last century. For example,

> the founders of Johns Hopkins University considered restricting study on that campus to graduate level only. In the end, some undergraduate education proved necessary, but the compromise was reluctantly made, and for many professors, class and lecture work became almost incidental. (p. 9)

Basic research became dominant after World War II because of the necessities demanded by that war. Boyer worried that too much emphasis was being placed on research to the exclusion of important aspects like teaching, as the above quote indicates. He concluded that we must change our mindset about what it meant to be a scholar, and he identified four areas of scholarship: discovery, integration, application, and teaching.

The Scholarship of Discovery

What Boyer meant by the scholarship of discovery was basic research. He felt that although too much emphasis was being placed on research, it was still an important aspect of scholarship. This form of scholarship contributes to human knowledge and also to the intellectual climate of a university.

The Scholarship of Integration

What Boyer meant by the scholarship of integration was the ability to connect facts from different disciplines to give meaning to one's findings. Thus, not only can one fit one's own research into the body of the existing literature, but one can also come to some conclusions about how this body of literature fits in with bodies of literature from different domains.

The Scholarship of Application

The scholarship of application is what Boyer referred to as "service" in phase two of the American college system. It examines how academic findings can be used to solve everyday problems. This is a two-way street, and it is assumed that the scholarship of application will also lead to the scholarship of discovery. Some of the more obvious examples of this form of scholarship are engineering, medicine, and architecture.

The Scholarship of Teaching

Finally, Boyer wanted to emphasize that good teaching is itself a form of scholarship. He felt that all too often, good teaching is marginalized or underappreciated, and noted that those who perform this task the best are often cited as the ones who have inspired other scholars to pursue their tasks:

> In the end, inspired teaching keeps the flame of scholarship alive. Almost all successful academics give credit to creative teachers—those mentors who define their work so compellingly that it became, for them, a lifetime challenge. (p. 24)

Boyer has had a long-standing interest in the scholarship of teaching. Earlier (Boyer, 1987), he had written on the need to constantly challenge oneself to improve one's teaching through change:

> Good teaching is at the heart of the undergraduate experience. All members of the faculty should work continually to improve the content of their courses and their methods of instruction. . . . The undergraduate

college, at its best, is an institution committed to knowledge, backed by wisdom—a place where students, through creative teaching, are encouraged to become intellectually engaged. With this vision, the great teacher is challenged not only to transmit information but also to enrich and inspire students, who will go on learning long after college days are over. (p. 159)

Although Boyer's interest was primarily in undergraduate teaching, his words should apply even more strongly to the graduate level. One of the principal components of graduate-level work is the scholarship of discovery. It is ironic that despite the fact that the only constant in graduate work is change (through the scholarship of discovery), some of our colleagues in the profession are reluctant to apply change to their own teaching methods. Even though multiculturalism is considered by many to be the "fourth force" in psychology (Pedersen, 1991, 1998; the "fourth dimension" in Sue et al.'s, 1998, wording), many of our mental health training colleagues have yet to discover this force or at least to apply it to their understanding of the discipline they have dedicated their lives to teaching.

☐ The Scholarship of Multiculturalism

If one were to look at multicultural teaching and training, one would see how such a discipline actually combines all four kinds of scholarship perhaps as well as, if not better than, any other area of psychology.

The Scholarship of Multicultural Discovery

It is daunting even to think of trying to list all of the areas in which multiculturalism has contributed to the scholarship of discovery. I have attempted to do so here, but I am certain that I have left out many important contributors in the area. As many are my friends, colleagues, and acquaintances, I hope the contributors I have not listed will forgive me. I have limited my discussion to only five areas in which multiculturalism has contributed to psychology's attempts at discovery.

Prejudice, Discrimination, and Racism

In the seminal book on this topic, Robert Guthrie's *Even the Rat was White* (Guthrie, 1976; 1998) discussed how the discipline of psychology was not immune to racism or to the colonial roots upon which this country was founded. As such, the discipline of psychology became—

unwittingly or not—an avenue for the continued promulgation of the notion of White supremacy. Thus, we had to reexamine studies that found racial and ethnic differences. As students of introductory statistics and methodology know, error variance is expected in studies, but systematic error variance biases results. Others contributing to this area have been Dovidio and Gaertner (1986), Jones (1972, 1997), Ponterotto and Pedersen (1993), Ridley (1995), Tatum (1997), and White (1984).

Stereotypes

Although some may group stereotypes with the above body of literature (Jones, 1997, identifies it as a mechanism of prejudice), I have decided to list it separately, as it has implications for nonracial issues as well as for racial issues. In my opinion, one of the more interesting recent studies in this area is Claude Steele's work on stereotype threats (e.g., Steele, 1997; Steele & Aronson, 1995). This work indicates that two groups of people with demonstrated equal ability to perform a task can be made to differ if one of the groups is led to believe that its performance may confirm a negative stereotype about that group. He conducted these studies using African Americans and Whites, who performed an extremely difficult verbal task, and using women and men, who performed an extremely difficult mathematical task. In both cases, when the stereotype was *not* primed, the groups were indistinguishable in performance, whereas when the stereotype *was* primed, the threatened group's performance went down significantly. Specifically, when the African American group was led to believe that its performance would affect perception of the intelligence of African Americans in general, its performance on the verbal task dropped precipitously, and when women were led to believe that their performance would indicate differences in the basic mathematical abilities of women and men, their performance dropped. Others who have contributed to our knowledge base about stereotypes have been Hamilton and Trolier (1986), Pettigrew (1979), and Sue and Okazaki (1990)

Identity

At least since the seminal work of Erik Erikson (e.g., Erikson, 1963, 1968), issues of identity have been of major concern in the psychological literature. Multiculturalism's contribution to this aspect of the scholarship of discovery has been in the area of racial identity. At the forefront has been Janet E. Helms (e.g., Helms, 1984, 1986, 1990, 1995). Building upon past work by Cross (1971) and Thomas (1971) on the sense of racial identity experienced by members of ethnic minorities, Helms has examined the responsibility of members of the White majority to develop their own sense of racial identity to meet ethnic minorities halfway (or at least, part of the way). In an era in which biracial and multiracial individuals are becoming more and more commonplace, Maria P. P. Root has been at the forefront in examining multiracial identity development (e.g., Root, 1992, 1996). So influential has her work been that she has even been sought out as a consultant by those organizing the United States government's year 2000 census on the issue of how to handle the multiracial category when collecting demographic information. Others who have conducted scholarly work in these areas are Carter (1990, 1995), Corvin and Wiggins (1989), Hall (1992, 1996), and Parham (1989).

Parenting Differences and Academic Achievement

In a seminal study, Baumrind (1971) made a distinction among authoritarian, permissive, and authoritative parenting styles. The authoritarian parenting style requires strict obedience to parental demands; the permissive parenting style allows children a great deal of freedom and provides very little parental direction; and the authoritative parenting style encourages a mutual communication pattern between parent and child, in which the parent is seen as an authority upon which the child can rely. Baumrind found that the authoritative parenting style was the only style that was related to academic achievement. Dornbusch and colleagues (e.g., Dornbusch, Prescott, & Ritter, 1987; Dornbusch, Ritter, Leiderman, Roberts, & Fraleigh, 1987; Ritter & Dornbusch, 1989) examined California high school students using the Baumrind (1971) distinctions among parenting styles. Dornbusch found that even though the original pattern—authoritative parenting styles being most closely associated with high academic achievement and authoritarian and permissive parenting styles being negatively related to academic achievement—was replicated for White, Black, and Hispanic/Latino populations, parenting style was unrelated to academic achievement among Asian students. Moreover, the authoritarian and permissive parenting styles were the *most* common styles among Asian parents. As Sue and Okazaki noted (1990), this result seems to be in conflict with the finding that Asian students attain far greater academic achievements than do their fellow students. Yee, Huang, and Lew (1998) cite other factors, such as culturally relevant norms of doing well in school as a reciprocal response to parental sacrifices (Wong, 1980) and attributions of effort (Stevenson & Stigler, 1992) as being explanatory of academic success of Asian students. Regardless of the interpretation, it is interesting that parenting styles deemed axiomatic as an explanation for academic achievement in the majority culture is unrelated to Asian success in education.

In another case of differing indicators of academic success, Sue and Abe (1988) reported that Asian/Pacific Islander and White freshman college students had similar grade point averages (GPA; 2.74 and 2.75, respectively). However, Scholastic Aptitude Test (SAT) scores in mathematics were by far a better predictor of GPA than were SAT verbal scores for Asian students, whereas SAT verbal scores were by far a better predictor of GPA than were SAT mathematic scores for White students. Again, indicators in one ethnic group do not necessarily translate to another ethnic group; the scholarship of multicultural discovery helps us to disentangle these differences.

Sexual Aggression

One of the standard models of sexual aggression has been the Confluence Model (Malamuth, Linz, Heavey, Barnes, & Acker, 1995; Malamuth, Sockloskie, Koss, & Tanaka, 1991). This model suggests that hostile masculinity and impersonal sex predict men's sexually aggressive behavior toward women. Hostile masculinity involves intrapersonal factors such as insecurity, defensiveness, hypersensitivity, hostile-distrustful orientation toward women, and gratification from controlling or dominating women. Impersonal sex involves engaging in sexual relations without closeness or commitment. Malamuth et al. (1995) reported the stability and predictive power of his Confluence Model over the 10-year period when he first proposed it.

Among Asians, collectivistic issues such as loss of face should be an important factor in predicting sexual aggression (see Ting-Toomey, 1994, and Zane, 1991, for discussions of "face"). Hall, Sue, Narang, and Lilly (1998) found that loss of face, an interpersonal factor, contributed to the ability to predict sexual aggression in Asian American male college students as opposed to their European American (White) counterparts. Asian American males who were concerned with loss of face had lower incidents of sexual aggression; concerns about loss of face were not at all predictive of European American male sexual aggression. However, the Confluence Model's intrapersonal factor was predictive of both Asian American and European American male sexual aggression.

The Scholarship of Multicultural Integration

Multiculturalism is by its very nature an integrative process, integrating not only a vast range of topics within the field of psychology but also reaching across domains to anthropology, sociology, and other disciplines in the social and behavioral sciences. Basic concepts such as the etic versus the emic approaches[1] to examining issues are direct descendants of anthropology, and individualism and collectivism are borrowed from sociology.

For example, one of the ackowledged experts in the field of research methodology was Donald T. Campbell. He recognized the difficulty and complexity of examining cross-national research, for even the simple question of the unit of analysis must be defined and is open to question (e.g., Campbell & Naroll, 1972). If one were to study societies, the society becomes the unit of analysis. What is the tribe or society being measured? Can different regions of a country be considered to represent different tribes? If there is a significant minority population within a society, does one measure samples from both populations and compare these samples with samples from a different society, giving each of the samples equal weight? Does one include some sort of hierarchical clustering within one society and use this clustering as the single representation of a society?

Once one gets past the difficulty of defining the unit of analysis, even more complex questions arise; the very definition of terms may come into question. For example, Triandis, Bontempo, Villareal, Asai, and Lucca (1988) discussed how the term "self-reliance" was interpreted differently in individualistic versus collectivistic societies. In individualistic societies, "self-reliance" meant the freedom to pursue one's own goals and to be in competition with others. In collectivistic societies, it meant not burdening the in-group, whereas competition was unrelated. Even the word "competition" had different connotations in these two societies. In individualistic societies, "competition" meant individuals would compete with one another, whereas in collectivistic societies, it meant that different in-groups would compete. As I have stated elsewhere (Mio & Iwamasa, 1993; Mio & Morris, 1990), Walter Mischel's famous series of studies on delay of gratification (Mischel, 1958, 1961) could be criticized on the basis of his misapplication of the terms "delay of gratification" and "adaptation" in interpreting results from children residing in ghettos. Mischel had one

---

[1]The etic approach is an attempt to build theory around the commonalities among cultures. However, quite often in the past, researchers would find results in one culture, then assume the results to be true across cultures. Berry (1969) terms this "imposed etics." The emic approach is a culturally sensitive attempt to understand terms that are relevant and meaningful within each culture. Triandis et al. (1986) and Mio and Morris (1990) further discuss the differences between the etic and emic approaches.

understanding of these terms, but they did not apply in the manner in which he had intended when he explained the behaviors of subjects residing in an inner-city environment.

These are only a few of the questions that multicultural scholars must address when conducting their research, applying research to the broader social context, and teaching about multicultural issues. The scholarship of integration is almost synonymous with multiculturalism.

The Scholarship of Multicultural Application

Through the scholarships of discovery and integration, certain understandings have emerged. Many have applied these understandings to the practice of service delivery to ethnic minority populations. Among the leaders in this area has been Nancy Boyd-Franklin (e.g., Boyd-Franklin, 1989; Hines & Boyd-Franklin, 1996). She has discussed how the realities of sociocultural environments have modified our understandings of ethnic minority populations and the way they are treated. For example, one of the realities in inner city African American families is that grandparents often are the primary caretakers of children. In fashioning family therapy, one must be prepared to conduct a three-generational intervention.

In applying theory to practice when conducting mental health services for American Indians, many have recommended that one first determine the degree to which the client feels acculturated into the larger society or remains affiliated with traditional American Indian values (e.g., Choney, Berryhill-Paapke, & Robbins, 1995; LaFromboise, 1988; LaFromboise, Trimble, & Mohatt, 1991; Trimble, Flemming, Beauvais, & Jumper-Thurman, 1996; Trimble & LaFromboise, 1985). Those strongly affiliated with traditional American Indian values may prefer to work also with a traditional (indigenous) healer (Choney, Berryhill-Paapke, & Robbins, 1995; LaFromboise, 1988). Based upon our experience in working with indigenous healers, there is a growing interest in the use of such indigenous healing techniques (Sue & Sue, 1999).

The Scholarship of Multicultural Teaching

The entire movement toward breaking down the barriers to integrating multicultural competencies into mental health training programs is an issue related to the scholarship of teaching. With the knowledge acquired through the scholarships of discovery, integration, and application, the next logical step is to integrate this knowledge into how we train our mental health professionals in the future. Although resistance to this integration comes in many forms, it is almost antithetical to university scholarship not to disseminate this knowledge as a matter of course.

It seems to me that the time has come for multiculturalism to break through the barriers of resistance and be integrated into every mental health training institution in the country. However, two questions arise: Why has it taken so long to take root? What is preventing it from flourishing at present? Modern forms of racism, with their covert and often undetectable nature, may be the reason resistance has not yet been overcome.

☐ The Multiculturalism of Scholarship

Boyer (1990) discussed the various ways in which scholarship should be conceptualized by professors and nonprofessors alike. I have attempted to argue that there is a scholarship of multiculturalism as well, and I have identified areas in which research in multicultural areas has contributed to our knowledge of the human condition. These contributions serve to underscore the multiculturalism of scholarship (acknowledgment to a reviewer for this term). Scholarship is the systematic pursuit of knowledge. To the extent that we live in a multicultural society in which both the subject and the researcher are multicultural, scholarship *must* recognize multiculturalism at its core. To ignore the multicultural components of scholarship is to conduct poor scholarship.

☐ References

Baumrind, D. (1971). Current patterns of parental authority. *Developmental Psychology Monograph, 4,* 1–103.

Bernal, M. E., & Padilla, A. M. (1982). Status of minority curricula and training in clinical psychology. *American Psychologist, 37,* 780–787.

Berry, J. W. (1969). On cross-cultural comparability. *International Journal of Psychology, 4,* 119–128.

Boyd-Franklin, N. (1989). *Black families in therapy: A multisystems approach.* New York: Guilford.

Boyer, E. L. (1987). *College: The undergraduate experience in America.* New York: Harper & Row.

Boyer, E. L. (1990). *Scholarship reconsidered: Priorities of the professoriate.* Princeton, NJ: The Carnegie Foundation for the Advancement of Teaching.

Boyer, E. L., & Hechinger, F. M. (1981). *Higher learning in the nation's service.* Washington, DC: The Carnegie Foundation for the Advancement of Teaching.

Campbell, D. T., & Naroll, R. (1972). The mutual methodological relevance of anthropology and psychology. In F. L. K. Hsu (Ed.), *Psychological anthropology* (pp. 435–463). Cambridge, MA: Schenkman.

Carter, R. T. (1990). The relationship between racism and racial identity among White Americans: An exploratory investigation. *Journal of Counseling and Development, 69,* 46–50.

Carter, R. T. (1995). *The influence of race and racial identity in psychotherapy.* New York: Wiley.

Choney, S. K., Berryhill-Paapke, E., & Robbins, R. R. (1995). The acculturation of American Indians: Developing frameworks for research and practice. In J. G. Ponterotto, J. M. Casas, L. A. Suzuki, & C. M. Alexander (Eds.), *Handbook of multicultural counseling* (pp. 73–92). Thousand Oaks, CA: Sage.

Corvin, S. A., & Wiggins, F. (1989). An antiracism training model for White professionals. *Journal of Multicultural Counseling and Development, 17,* 105–112.

Cross, W. E., Jr. (1971). The Negro-to-Black conversion experience: Toward a psychology of Black liberation. *Black World, 20,* 13–27.

Dornbusch, S. M., Prescott, B. L., & Ritter, P. L. (1987, April). *The relation of high school academic performance and student effort to language use and recency of migration among Asian- and Pacific-Americans.* Paper presented at the meeting of the American Educational Research Association, Washington, DC.

Dornbusch, S. M., Ritter, P. L., Leiderman, P. H., Roberts, D. F., & Fraleigh, M. J. (1987). The relation of parenting style to adolescent school performance. *Child Development, 55,* 1244–1257.

Dovidio, J. F., & Gaertner, S. L. (1986). Prejudice, discrimination, and racism: Historical trends and contemporary approaches. In J. F. Dovidio & S. L. Gaertner (Eds.), *Prejudice, discrimination, and racism* (pp. 1–34). Orlando, FL: Academic Press.

Erikson, E. H. (1963). *Childhood and society* (2nd ed.). New York: Norton.

Erikson, E. H. (1968). *Identity: Youth and crisis.* Toronto: Norton.

Guthrie, R. V. (1976). *Even the rat was White.* New York: Harper & Row.

Guthrie, R. V. (1998). *Even the rat was White* (2nd ed.). Boston: Allyn & Bacon.

Hall, C. C. I. (1992). Please choose one: Ethnic identity choices for biracial individuals. In M. P. P. Root (Ed.), *Racially mixed people in America* (pp. 250–264). Newbury Park, CA: Sage.

Hall, C. C. I. (1996). 2001: A race odyssey. In M. P. P. Root (Ed.), *The multiracial experience* (pp. 395–410). Thousand Oaks, CA: Sage.

Hall, G. C. N., Sue, S., Narang, D. S., & Lilly, R. S. (1998, August). Culture-specific models of men's sexual aggression: Intra- and interpersonal determinants. In B. P. Marx (Chair), *Prevention of sexual assault: Current status and future directions.* Symposium presented at the 106th annual convention of the American Psychological Association, San Francisco.

Hamilton, D. L., & Trolier, T. K. (1986). Stereotypes and stereotyping: An overview of the cognitive approach. In J. F. Dovidio & S. L. Gaertner (Eds.), *Prejudice, discrimination, and racism* (pp. 127–163). Orlando, FL: Academic Press.

Helms, J. T. (1984). Toward a theoretical model of the effects of race on counseling: A Black and White model. *Counseling Psychologist, 12,* 153–165.

Helms, J. T. (1986). Expanding racial identity theory to cover counseling process. *Journal of Counseling Psychology, 33,* 62–64.

Helms, J. T. (1990). *Black and White racial identity: Theory, research, and practice.* New York: Greenwood.

Helms, J. T. (1995). An update of Helms's White and people of color racial identity models. In J. G. Ponterotto, J. M. Casas, L. A. Suzuki, & C. M. Alexander (Eds.), *Handbook of multicultural counseling* (pp. 181–191). Thousand Oaks, CA: Sage.

Hines, P. M., & Boyd-Franklin, N. (1996). African American families. In M. McGoldrick, J. Giordano, & J. K. Pearce (Eds.), *Ethnicity & family therapy* (2nd ed., pp. 66–84). New York: Guilford.

Jones, J. M. (1972). *Prejudice and racism.* Reading, MA: Addison-Wesley.

Jones, J. M. (1997). *Prejudice and racism* (2nd ed.). New York: McGraw-Hill.

LaFromboise, T. D. (1988). American Indian mental health policy. *American Psychologist, 43,* 388–397.

LaFromboise, T. D., Trimble, J. E., & Mohatt, G. V. (1991). Counseling intervention and American Indian tradition: An integrative approach. *The Counseling Psychologist, 18,* 628–654.

Mio, J. S. (1989). Experiential involvement as an adjunct to teaching cultural sensitivity. *Journal of Multicultural Counseling and Development, 17,* 38–46.

Mio, J. S., & Iwamasa, G. Y. (1993). To do, or not to do: That is the question for White cross-cultural researchers. *The Counseling Psychologist, 21,* 197–212.

Mio, J. S., & Morris, D. R. (1990). Cross-cultural issues in psychology training programs: An invitation for discussion. *Professional Psychology: Research and Practice, 21,* 434–441.

Mischel, W. (1958). Preference for delayed reinforcement: An experimental study of a cultural observation. *Journal of Abnormal and Social Psychology, 56,* 57–61.

Mischel, W. (1961). Delay of gratification, need for achievement, and acquiescence in another culture. *Journal of Abnormal and Social Psychology, 62,* 543–552.

Parham, T. A. (1989). Cycles of psychological Nigrescence. *The Counseling Psychologist, 17,* 187–226.

Pedersen, P. B. (1991). Multiculturalism as a fourth force in counseling [Special issue]. *Journal of Counseling and Development, 70.*

Pedersen, P. B. (Ed.). (1998). *Multiculturalism as a fourth force.* Philadelphia: Taylor & Francis.

Pettigrew, T. F. (1979). The ultimate attribution error: Extending Allport's cognitive analysis of prejudice. *Personality and Social Psychology Bulletin, 5,* 461–476.

Ponterotto, J. G., & Pedersen, P. B. (1993). *Preventing prejudice: A guide for counselors and educators.* Newbury Park, CA: Sage.

Ponterotto, J. G., & Sabanini, H. B. (1989). "Classics" in multicultural counseling: A systematic 5-year content analysis. *Journal of Multicultural Counseling and Development, 17,* 23–37.

Ridley, C. R. (1995). *Overcoming unintentional racism in counseling and therapy: A practitioner's guide to intentional intervention.* Thousand Oaks, CA: Sage.

Ritter, P. L., & Dornbusch, S. M. (1989, March). *Ethnic variation in family influences on academic achievement.* Paper presented at the American Educational Research Association Meeting, San Francisco.

Root, M. P. P. (1992). Within, between, and beyond race. In M. P. P. Root (Ed.), *Racially mixed people in America* (pp. 3–11). Newbury Park, CA: Sage.

Root, M. P. P. (1996). A bill of rights for racially mixed people. In M. P. P. Root (Ed.), *The multiracial experience: Racial borders as the new frontier* (pp. 3–14). Thousand Oaks, CA: Sage.

Steele, C. M. (1997). A threat in the air: How stereotypes shape intellectual identity and performance. *American Psychologist, 52,* 613–629.

Steele, C. M., & Aronson, J. (1995). Stereotype threat and the intellectual test performance of African Americans. *Journal of Personality and Social Psychology, 69,* 797–811.

Stevenson, H. W., & Stigler, J. W. (1992). *The learning gap: Why our schools are failing and what we can learn from Japanese and Chinese education.* New York: Simon & Schuster.

Sue, D. W. (1981). *Counseling the culturally different*. New York: Wiley.

Sue, D. W., Arredondo, P., & McDavis, R. J. (1992). Multicultural competencies/standards: A pressing need. *Journal of Counseling and Development, 70,* 477–486.

Sue, D. W., Bernier, J. B., Durran, M., Feinberg, L., Pedersen, P., Smith, E., & Vasquez-Nuttall, E. (1982). Position paper: Cross-cultural counseling competencies. *The Counseling Psychologist, 10,* 45–52.

Sue, D. W., Carter, R. T., Casas, J. M., Fouad, N. A., Ivey, A. E., Jensen, M., LaFromboise, T., Manese, J. E., Ponterotto, J. G., & Vasquez-Nuttall, E. (1998). *Multicultural counseling competencies: Individual and organizational development.* Thousand Oaks, CA: Sage.

Sue, D. W., & Sue, D. (1999). *Counseling the culturally different* (3rd ed.). New York: Wiley.

Sue, S. (1977). Community mental health services to minority groups: Some optimism, some pessimism. *American Psychologist, 32,* 616–624.

Sue, S., & Abe, J. (1988). *Predictors of academic achievement among Asian American and White students* (College Board Report No. 88-11). New York: College Entrance Examination Board.

Sue, S., & Okazaki, S. (1990). Asian American educational achievements: A phenomenon in search of an explanation. *American Psychologist, 45,* 913–920.

Tatum, B. D. (1997). *"Why are all the Black kids sitting together in the cafeteria?" and other conversations about race.* New York: Basic Books.

Thomas, C. W. (1971). *Boys no more.* Beverly Hills, CA: Glencoe.

Ting-Toomey, S. (Ed.). (1994). *The challenge of facework.* Albany, NY: State University of New York Press.

Triandis, H. C., Bontempo, R., Blatancourt, H., Bond, M., Leung, K., Brenes, A., Georgas, J., Wui, C. H., Marin, G., Setiadi, B., Sinha, J. B. P., Verma, J., Spangenberg, J., Touzard, H., & de Montmollin, G. (1986). The measurement of etic aspects of individualism and collectivism across cultures. *Australian Journal of Psychology* (special issue on cross-cultural psychology), *38,* 257–267.

Triandis, H. C., Bontempo, R., Villareal, M. J., Asai, M., & Lucca, N. (1988). Individualism and collectivism: Cross-cultural perspectives on self-ingroup relationships. *Journal of Personality and Social Psychology, 54,* 323–338.

Trimble, J. E., Flemming, C. M., Beauvais, F., & Jumper-Thurman, P. (1996). Essential cultural and social strategies for counseling Native American Indians. In P. B. Pedersen, J. G. Draguns, W. J. Lonner, & J. E. Trimble (Eds.), *Counseling across cultures* (4th ed., pp. 177–209). Thousand Oaks, CA: Sage.

Trimble, J. E., & LaFromboise, T. (1985). American Indians and the counseling process: Culture, adaptation, and style. In P. Pedersen (Ed.), *Handbook of cross-cultural counseling and therapy* (pp. 127–134). Westport, CT: Greenwood.

White, J. L. (1984). *The psychology of Blacks: An Afro-American perspective.* Englewood Cliffs, NJ: Prentice Hall.

Wong, M. (1980). Model students? Teachers' perceptions and expectations of their Asian and White students. *Sociology of Education, 53,* 236–246.

Yee, B. W. K., Huang, L. N., & Lew, A. (1998). Families: Life-span socialization in a cultural context. In L. C. Lee & N. W. S. Zane (Eds.), *Handbook of Asian American psychology* (pp. 83–135). Thousand Oaks, CA: Sage.

Zane, N. (1991, August). *An empirical examination of loss of face among Asian Americans.* Paper presented at the 99th annual convention of the American Psychological Association, San Francisco.

Covert Racism and the Subtlety of Modern Resistance

I took my 18-month-old son to a [daycare center] near my house last month to check out the environment. I put him down on the floor, and he saw another 18-month-old boy a few feet away. He toddled over to him to give him a hug and a kiss. Well, you know how unsteady 18-month-olds are. When he tried to hug the other boy, they both kind of tumbled onto the floor and they started to cry. Immediately, the boy's mother and a daycare worker rushed over to the boys to separate them. Excitedly, the daycare worker turned to me and asked, "Does he bite?" A few minutes later, two White girls were interlocked in combat, with each pulling the other's hair. These two girls were screaming bloody murder, but the same daycare worker was gently saying things like, "It's all right," "She didn't mean to hurt you," "Please let go," "It'll be okay," and so forth. I thought, "Well, if they are going to treat Black kids and White kids so differently, I'm not going to let my son be exposed to such an environment. I made a decision right then and there to find a different daycare center for my son."

Shelly Harrell (personal communication, August 1997)

Most of us are familiar with images of racism. Such images include American Indians being nearly wiped out by the genocide of last century, Ku Klux Klansmen posing for pictures after a lynching, Japanese Americans having nearly all of their worldly possessions confiscated and being imprisoned during World War II just because of their genetic Japanese heritage, Bull Connor and his police dogs and billy clubs suppressing African Americans who were nonviolently asking for their rights, fire hoses blasting away at African American protesters, George Wallace standing in the doorway of a school to prevent African American elementary school children from registering for school, Mexican Americans being rounded up by Immigration and Naturalization Service agents just because of the color of their skin. These images are seared in our minds as icons of American racism. More modern images of racism include that of Rodney King being beaten with nightsticks by five Los Angeles policemen, David Duke—a former Grand Wizard of the Ku Klux Klan—being nominated for governor by a major United States political party, Yusef Hawkins being shot to death in New York City because he was walking in a White neighborhood and someone thought he was the African American man dating a woman from that neighborhood, Patrick J. Buchanan, a major candidate for the Republican Party's presidential nomination in 1992 and 1996, suggesting that we place racially charged and life-threatening symbols on the border between the United States and Mexico saying things like, "This is a warning to you, Jose, to stay out of our country," the horrific murder of James Byrd, Jr., in Jasper, Texas, by three White supremacists who dragged Mr. Byrd for miles behind their pickup truck . . . these are reminders to us that racism still exists. However, because we do not engage in such activities—and we might even condemn them—we are able to live with safety in knowledge that we ourselves are not racists.

Crispin Sartwell (1998), in writing about the murdering of Byrd by dragging him behind the pickup truck, stated that White America needs such incidents of bigotry so that it can go along deploring such incidents in order to feel nonracist. He writes:

> Average white people don't think that they are racists. Because they would never utter the "n-word" or eat in segregated restaurants or teach their children explicitly that black people are inferior, they believe that they cannot be prejudiced. When public opinion surveys are taken, almost no one responds with what are considered to be racist views, which has led some "experts" to conclude that Americans have overcome their legacy of racial injustice. . . . [However,] (t)he basic racism of American culture has not even been addressed, much less solved. Everyone should deplore Byrd's lynching. But it is easy to deplore lynching. It is much harder to do anything about the central, subtle racism that surrounds us. (p. M-5)

☐ Ridley's Conceptualization of Racism

Imagine yourself watching television when two consecutive commercials depict an African American as the central character. If these were not sports commercials, would your immediate thought be, "Gosh, they are sure promoting a lot of Blacks on TV"? However, when two or three (or ten) consecutive commercials depict White individuals as the central characters, do you ever wonder, "Why is it that they have so many Whites on TV"? This thought about African Americans (or other identifiable ethnic minorities) indicates what might be considered to be covert, unintentional racism.

Charles Ridley (1989, 1995) presented a conceptualization of racism that can be applied to individuals or to institutions. This conceptualization identifies three forms of racism that can occur at the individual or institutional level: (1) overt, intentional racism; (2) covert, intentional racism; and (3) covert, unintentional racism.

Overt, intentional racism is the form of racism that is of the Ku Klux Klan variety, where it is clearly racist and recognizable by all. The protagonist is aware of his or her behavior and is intending the behavior to hurt a person or group of people. This form of racism does not need to be further delineated. We all know what it is.

Covert, intentional racism is hidden racism. It is expressed when an individual (or institution) wants to act in a racist manner but tries to disguise it so that it can operate undetected. I lived in Chicago during the days after the infamous Mayor Richard Daley ruled the city. It was discovered that the Chicago public school system was woefully in debt because it had 25% too many schools, given the student population. Many said that the reason there were so many schools, was that Mayor Daley had become concerned whenever African American areas began to intrude upon White areas. In order to keep the resultant integration from taking place, he built another school in the African American area under the guise of doing them a favor by giving them new facilities. I cannot confirm the veracity of this explanation of why there were so many public schools in Chicago. I can only say that there were, in fact, 25% more schools than were needed, and that these extra schools were in predominantly African American areas. But if racism was the real reason, this would be a clear example of covert, intentional racism.

Covert, unintentional racism is a form of racism that comes about because of laws or traditions that are racist in nature, but the protagonist is unaware of the racist roots of these laws or traditions. An excellent example of this situation is the famous incident in which the Los Angeles Dodgers' General Manager, Al Campanis, said on national television that Blacks did not have the "necessities" to become baseball managers or general managers. He was given the opportunity to retract or amend his statement, but because he was unaware of the racist nature of his words, he only made the situation worse. Mr. Campanis was immediately fired from the Dodgers for making such inflammatory statements. Dr. Harry Edwards, a famous University of California, Berkeley, sociologist, whose life work is in the area of eliminating racial barriers, especially in college and professional athletics, worked with Mr. Campanis as a result of the above incident. Dr. Edwards said that after working on a variety of issues to improve race relations, he was convinced that Mr. Campanis was not a racist, he was simply naive in his understanding of racial issues. Mr. Campanis naively repeated and perpetuated racist stereotypes that were widespread in the world of baseball.

At the risk of exposing myself as an unintentional racist (at least in my younger days), I recall a conversation I had with a high school friend. We were wondering who would be quarterback for the high school the following year, after Vince Ferragamo graduated. (I was in Ferragamo's graduating class, but I was worried for my friend's class the next year.) He suggested the name of an African American at the school, and I asked, "How could he be quarterback?" My friend said that this guy had a great arm, was fast, and could make quick decisions, but I still wondered how he could be quarterback. I had heard that Blacks could not be quarterbacks, and I blindly accepted this view, not knowing why people were saying such things. I played high school basketball, and I knew the athleticism and quick decision-making of my Black teammates, but no one had ever told me that Blacks could not play basketball. In fact, I *knew* that Blacks could play basketball, for Elgin Baylor was one of my favorite basketball players back then, and he was widely regarded as one of the best basketball players of all time. However, I did not know that Blacks could become quarterbacks, as there were no professional Black quarterbacks at that time and very few on major college football teams. Boy, was I naive! Ridley (1995) wrote about people like Al Campanis and me:

> Unintentional behavior is perhaps the most insidious form of racism. Unintentional racists are unaware of the harmful consequences of their behavior. They may be well-intentioned, and on the surface, their behavior may appear to be responsible. Because individuals, groups, or institutions that engage in unintentional racism do not wish to do harm, it is difficult to get them to see themselves as racist. They are more likely to deny their racism. (p. 38)

My self-perception is that I am more aware than most people about issues of race, and that if something that I think or do is pointed out as unintentionally racist, I will immediately attempt to eliminate it from my repertoire of responses. However, I am self-aware enough to know that I have to be continually vigilant, or my covert, unintentional racism will, as Ridley suggests, become insidiously ingrained in me.

Given my state of awareness about such issues, I have enough insight to know that it must be very difficult for those with less awareness to be convinced of the underlying racism in their thoughts or actions. Shelly Harrell's potential daycare worker would probably deny that she had a racist bone in her body and would insist that her question about the "eating habits" of Shelly's son was simply a point of information. However, had Dr. Harrell's son been exposed to a daily environment of such subtle racism, he may very well have internalized the oppression (Tatum, 1997) and as an adult he would accept and operate by the absorbed rules and stereotypical categories that he had learned to use as definitions of what it means to be an African American male.

☐ Covert, Intentional Racism in the Broader Social Context

> Cultural racism—the cultural images and messages that affirm the assumed superiority of Whites and the assumed inferiority of people of color—is like smog in the air. Sometimes it is so thick it is visible, other times it is less apparent, but always, day in and day out, we are breathing it. None of us would introduce ourselves as "smog-breathers" (and most of us don't want to be described as prejudiced), but if we live in a smoggy place, how can we avoid breathing the air? (p. 6)
>
> Beverly Daniel Tatum (1997)

Because covert, unintentional racism is so insidious, it is important to be able to recognize it, expose it, and work on ourselves and others to eliminate it. For the rest of this chapter, I discuss such racism as I have encountered it. In so doing, I hope to sensitize readers so they can detect this form of racism in their own lives.

Covert, Unintentional Racism at the Departmental Level

My first awareness of covert, unintentional racism occurred when I was in my very first academic position in the Department of Counseling at California State University, Fullerton. I hesitate to mention this, because the unintended consequences turned out to be quite positive for me. However, at the time of its occurrence, it placed me under a great deal of stress.

I was a junior faculty member in a department whose responsibility was to train master's level mental health workers. The State of

California had recently required that such students take a course in multicultural issues. Our newly hired faculty member was to teach this course but, unfortunately, this individual decided at the last minute not to join our department. His dissertation was taking him much longer to complete than he had anticipated, and he reasoned that if he decided to teach in our department, with its requirement of teaching four courses each semester, he would not finish his dissertation for quite some time. The Thursday before classes were to begin on the following Monday, my department chair asked—no, assigned—me to teach the cross-cultural issues course that the new hire was supposed to have taught. Dutifully, I agreed to do so, and I added this new preparation to that for the other three courses I was to teach. Needless to say, it was not a fun semester for me.

As I had mentioned, the long-term consequences turned out to be positive for me, as my work in the multicultural area has been my most rewarding academic endeavor. However, there was no reason in the world for me to teach this course other than covert, unintentional racism. Even though I received my Ph.D. in an era when I was *supposed* to have had training in multicultural issues, in fact, I had never taken such a course, as my department did not even offer such a course (see my discussion in Chapter 1 on this, based upon the Bernal and Padilla, 1982, article). I had not read extensively in the area, as my dissertation had concerned an application of cognitive psychology theories to detecting thought disorder on Rorschach protocols. It was only the second year of my first academic position, and with four courses to teach each semester, I had little time to read in areas outside of my teaching preparation. Apparently, the only "qualification" I had to teach this course was that I was a faculty member who was also a member of an ethnic minority. I will come back to this point after I discuss the next incident of covert, unintentional racism. I want to underscore how covert and unintentional this racist incident was. I was on very friendly terms with the department chair, and she even apologized for having to make this assignment. However, she did not dare to assign it to any of the White faculty members in the department, and she was not on friendly grounds with another ethnic minority faculty member, who would have resisted this assignment.

My next position was in the Department of Psychology at Washington State University. As most academics know, one of the requirements involved in earning a doctoral degree is to successfully complete a preliminary examination. During my first year in the department, those who were involved with students' prelim exams gathered together for a meeting to discuss the students' performance and to decide whether or not to pass each student. One very senior professor criticized the performance of an ethnic minority student. He said that although her overall performance was acceptable, he was quite disappointed in a section in which he had asked her to discuss how the literature on cross-cultural issues might address the topic (I believe it was psychopathology). Despite the fact that such articles did not exist on her approved prelim list and that she was primarily responsible for the raising of her five children in her very traditional marriage, this professor seemed to think that just because of her ethnic minority status, she should have been aware of the literature pertaining to ethnic minorities. Again, as I mentioned in Chapter 1, a course on this topic did not exist in the department until I developed it (and its first offering was two years *after* this student's prelim). Therefore, one wonders how in the world this student would have been able to prepare for such a question. I am certain that this professor thought he was doing her a favor by asking about cross-cultural issues, demonstrating to her how sensitive he was in recognizing the importance of the area. The fact remains that his behavior was covertly and unintentionally racist. Both this student and I were somehow supposed to know about the literature simply because of our status as members of ethnic minority groups.

Covert, Unintentional Racism in the Profession

In many respects, this entire book is an attempt to address covert, unintentional racism in the profession of psychology and the larger system of academia. Certainly, the seven deadly resistances identified in the Sue et al. (1998) book and discussed in Chapter 1 are often uttered by well-intentioned but unintentionally racist individuals. As these seven resistances were addressed before, I will not address them here. However, this chapter would be incomplete if I do not address at least a couple of instances that demonstrate that the profession of psychology still has a long way to go to eliminate covert, unintentional racism.

Korchin (1980) related a story that demonstrated the profession's insensitivity to ethnic minority issues. He and a colleague were attempting to publish a study comparing successful and unsuccessful African American college students. This study found some important differences, but one of the reviewers rejected the study. "In the opinion of one consulting editor, the study was 'grievously flawed'—there was no white control group" (Korchin, 1980, p. 263). Given that this was a study that examined subgroups of African American college students, it is curious that the reviewer would have made such a comment; he or she must have been blindly following a covert, unintentionally racist dictum that states that no study is important unless it contains White participants. As Korchin put it, "What would happen, might we suppose, if someone submitted a study identical in all respects except that all subjects were white? Would it be criticized because it lacked a black control group?" (p. 263).

Sue (1998, 1999) discussed the Korchin experience within the broader framework of the tension between internal and external validity. As most psychologists know, in research, the tighter the controls one employs to address internal validity, the less externally valid the results. On the other hand, the more one attempts to address concerns about the external validity and generalizability, the more threats to internal validity one encounters because of uncontrolled variables. As Campbell and Stanley (1963) put it in their classic book on research design, "Both types of criteria are obviously important, even though they are frequently at odds in that features increasing one may jeopardize the other" (p. 5). Thus, researchers must find a balance between these two pressures. However, Sue (1998, 1999) argued that the overwhelming majority of those who review manuscripts and conduct studies forget the demands of external validity in favor of tight internal controls. Therefore, the reviewer of Korchin's manuscript rejected it because of a blind adherence to internal validity. As most studies dealing with ethnic minority populations are attempts to reflect the realities of the external world, such studies are naturally concerned with the pressures of external validity and so are disadvantaged in the eyes of reviewers not accustomed to taking such variables into account.

Another evidence of covert, unintentional racism is revealed by a situation I witnessed. I feel this situation epitomizes the type of insensitivity that is prevalent among well-meaning individuals who may act in such unintentionally racist ways.

As most who are reading this book know, the president of the American Psychological Association (APA) in 1998 was Martin Seligman. Dr. Seligman is legendary for his past work on learned helplessness (e.g., Abramson, Seligman, & Teasdale, 1978; Seligman, 1968, 1975; Seligman, Rossellini, & Kozak, 1975) and his newer work on learned optimism (e.g., Seligman, 1991, 1998). Clearly, he is one of the giants in the field of psychology. His new initiative may be most influential and have a strong impact not only on the field of psychology but also on the world stage: ethnopolitical warfare.

I had been elected a member of one of the APA's governance groups, the Committee for Ethnic Minority Affairs (CEMA) for the years 1998 to 2000. This committee meets twice a year along with all of the other governing committees of APA. My first meeting was in the spring of

1998. Dr. Seligman came to visit our meeting to show his support for the committee and also to discuss his new initiative on ethnopolitical warfare. Events such as the Holocaust during World War II and more recent events such as the holocaust in Rwanda and the ethnoreligious fighting in the Balkans convinced Dr. Seligman that something was needed to address such issues and avoid bloodshed in generations to come. He said that throughout his career, he had had to beg for money by fighting with his dean or university for departmental support, by applying for private and government grants, and so forth. However, when he began to inform foundations and other agencies about his plans to start a branch of psychology (or even a brand new discipline) concerned with ethnopolitical warfare, "this was the first time in my life that such agencies asked me how much they can contribute to such an enterprise." Money was flowing into his cause. As a first step toward this new discipline, he had organized the first-ever ethnopolitical warfare conference in Derry, Northern Ireland, both as a symbol of ethnopolitical healing and as an encouragement of rapprochement between the Protestants and Catholics in the region. He proudly talked about how many world experts he had invited to the conference and the abundant funds that had been contributed.

Clearly as an afterthought, and realizing the makeup of the audience to which he was speaking, Dr. Seligman quickly added that anyone on the committee was welcome to attend the conference, "but you had better hurry up and register because there is limited space in Derry." One of the committee members, Sandra K. Choney, asked where she could apply for funds to attend the conference. Dr. Seligman said, "You will have to get there on your own funds. The money is spent." Dr. Choney, a woman who gave up an academic position at a major university to live on an American Indian reservation and work with her tribe, tried to explain that some committee members were earning limited funds and could not afford to fly to Ireland and pay for a week's worth of hotel expenses, so they needed help if they were to attend the conference. Another committee member, Roberto Velasquez, tried to get Dr. Seligman to understand how ethnopolitical warfare has happened right here in the United States, as the American Indian population was nearly wiped out by Whites who wanted to expand westward and settle in land occupied by the indigenous people. It was important for a conference of this type to hear from those whose history has been directly relevant to the very topic of discussion. Again, Dr. Seligman said, "The money is spent." I said, "But I thought you said that this was the first time in your lifetime that funding agencies were asking you how much they could contribute to this worthy cause, so surely there must be *some* money available for one or two CEMA committee members so they can attend the conference, if your offer for us to attend was sincere." Again, Dr. Seligman said, "The money for this conference is spent," and he quickly ended the meeting.

After Dr. Seligman left, the four senior committee members said that he had made essentially the same speech the previous fall, and CEMA committee members had tried to impress upon him how insulting it was for American ethnic minority communities to be excluded from endeavors such as this. For years, ethnic minority scholars have been talking about such issues as the genocide of many ethnic minority communities right here in the United States (e.g., Choney, Berryhill-Paapke, & Robbins, 1995; Comas-Díaz, 1994; Richardson, 1981; Rosewater, 1990). However, it seems that White Americans find it difficult to face up to this history. Instead, it seems to be much easier to focus on the genocide and atrocities of ethnic minorities in other countries (Parham, 1990) and take in White expertise to try to understand these issues. However, those who had attended the previous meeting with Dr. Seligman thought that they had made an impression when they asked him to take seriously the notion that ethnic minority researchers in the United States have some expertise in ethnopolitical warfare. Apparently, they did not make such an impression. Repeated attempts to effect change in Dr. Seligman led only to frustration and negative results. The irony was not lost on anyone in the room. The target of these efforts was the father of learned helplessness.

I do not relate this story to publically embarrass Dr. Seligman, but if this is what it takes to get him to finally acknowledge the potential contribution of American ethnic minorities to his pet project, I will gladly sacrifice any future positive relationship I may have with him to further the cause of multiculturalism. However, I feel that this is a prime example of how someone as brilliant as Dr. Seligman can have cultural blinders on when it comes to multicultural issues. I feel that Dr. Seligman's new discipline may very well have a major impact on the world, and I applaud him for his vision in this area. To the extent that the entire psychological community can support his efforts, the probability of the success of his endeavor increases; to the extent that he continues to alienate large factions of the psychological community, the impact of his initiative lessens. CEMA's response to his initiative did not seem to make a large enough impression on him, as his plenary address to the entire assembly of governance committees of APA soon after his meeting with CEMA continued to include the language of White colonialism trying to solve the problems of troubled countries throughout the rest of the world. Thus, intelligence and even exposure to the issues of multiculturalism are not enough to overcome the years of resistance and counterarguments to which we are exposed. Resistance is in the air that we breathe. As I stated above, even though I am more aware of these issues than most people, I still lapse into moments when I am unaware of the smog.

I might add that Dr. Seligman may need to be more sensitive to gender issues as well as to multiculturalism in order to receive the broad band of support he desires for his new initiative on ethnopolitical warfare. In the opening chapter of his book *Learned Optimism* (Seligman, 1991), Dr. Seligman wrote in a footnote:

> Throughout this book, when the pronoun "he" is used, as it is in this sentence, simply to mean a human being, the reader is asked to read it as "he or she." To use "he or she" in every instance would be awkward and distracting, and at the moment there seems to be no workable alternative, although in due time the ever vigorous English language will doubtless evolve one. (p. 6)

This footnote accompanied an 11-sentence paragraph in which he used the words "he" and "his" nine times within a space of four consecutive sentences. The surprising thing about this is that APA had adopted a position over a decade earlier to replace the sexist language to which Dr. Seligman's footnote refers, and it has published guidelines for alternative language at least since 1978 (American Psychological Association, 1978). Interestingly, by the time of the reprinting of *Learned Optimism* (Seligman, 1998), Dr. Seligman—who was by then president of the APA—was still holding onto his original sexist language despite the fact that he had rewritten the forward and two decades had passed since the APA had first published its guidelines.

Covert, Unintentional Racism in Society

Now it is time to examine the air we breathe. In many respects, this might be the most difficult section to write because there is so much I could discuss, I cannot cover it all. In my discussion of a few incidents I have noticed, I will point out the subtle examples of covert, unintentional racism in society that I discuss with my students. These examples are not dramatic but insidious, and they are primarily media-driven.

Let me turn from ethnopolitical warfare to a related topic: political violence within countries. In my observations of news stories, I notice that White reporters are continually referring to political violence between factions of Blacks as "Black-on-Black violence." When supporters of ousted President Jean Bertrand Aristide of Haiti suspected people within their neighborhoods of being informants to the military junta that forced President Aristide out of the country, they engaged in "necklacing," a horrible practice of placing a tire soaked in gasoline around the neck of the informant and setting the tire on fire. The press showed these rituals on worldwide television, calling it Black-on-Black violence. When Nelson Mandela was released from prison, and it looked like a Black leader might be the next president of South Africa, there were many clashes between Mandela's African National Congress Party and Zulu Chief Butelezi's Inkhata Freedom Party. At times, these clashes turned into violent ones, and again, the international press referred to it as Black-on-Black violence. However, whenever there was a clash between supporters of the Irish Republican Army and the Ulster Unionists in Northern Ireland, I did not hear one international correspondent refer to it as White-on-White violence. The entire war in Bosnia-Herzegovina was between White ethnic Europeans, yet again, no reference to it as White-on-White violence could be heard in the international press. Were these reporters blatantly racist? I would suspect not. However, their reporting certainly reflected covert, unintentional racism.

In the United States, the drug problem is often depicted as a Black (or minority) problem. Certainly, whenever news stories want to illustrate the drug problem, they show "shooting galleries" in inner cities where collections of individuals are injecting heroin into their veins, or they show the sale of drugs on inner-city street corners or inmates imprisoned for drug abuse. Nearly every one of the offenders has black or brown skin. Words are not needed; the pictures tell the story. Or do they? One reason images of inner-city shooting galleries are shown is because it is easy to do so. These individuals typically do not have the ability to refuse such stories, or they can be bought off very easily because of their financial circumstances. On the other hand, if such news stories attempted to show drug use in White suburban settings, threats of lawsuits and court injunctions would surely follow. Pictures of drug sales on inner-city street corners are easily obtained through telephoto lenses, whereas such scenes are not typically available in White suburbs because of the increased police protection enjoyed by suburban communities. It is easy to show Black and brown faces in prison drug programs because for ethnic minority communities, the drug problem is considered a law enforcement problem, but for White communities, the drug problem is considered a mental health problem, and mental health settings enjoy much more confidentiality than do prison settings. Ethnic minorities who abuse drugs are sent to prison, whereas their White counterparts are sent to drug rehabilitation programs. Despite this disparity in the way in which ethnic minorities and their White counterparts are treated at the last stage of the criminal justice system, Whites still constitute the great majority of arrests for drugs in this country—67% (Federal Bureau of Investigation, 1997).

William Bennett, the "Drug Czar" under the Bush Administration, underscored the above points when he was in office. On a number of occasions during interviews on television, he cited statistics provided by his office that indicated that the White majority in this country was being given the false idea that the drug problem was mainly an inner-city, ethnic minority problem. He stated that 95% of all African Americans living in the inner city do *not* abuse drugs and that 75% to 85% of all abusers of drugs (whether they are arrested or not) are White. In thinking that drug use occurs primarily in the inner city among ethnic minorities, Whites have failed to understand how their indifference to the problem has led to policies that are ineffective in dealing with drug abuse in the United States.

Another aspect of covert, unintentional racism involves acts of omission as opposed to acts of comission. People experience crime as an ethnic minority issue because the media reports things like "Black gang violence," "Latino gang violence," and "Asian gang violence." Such reports do not protect the larger African American, Latino, and Asian communities from suspicion. Whenever Whites are involved in gang activities, they are characterized as "The Mafia" or "White supremacists," thus allowing the average White citizen to be protected from incrimination, safe in the knowledge that he or she is not in the Mafia or involved with the White supremacist movement. I have heard countless African American males relate stories of how they are offended when they pass a White woman who not-so-subtlely clutches her purse more tightly or even avoids close contact by crossing the street instead of walking by the "threatening" figure. However, a little-known statistic reveals that the overwhelming majority of child molesters are White. West and Templer (1994) reported that more than 91% (83 of 91) of the incarcerations in the state of Nevada for child molestation were of White perpetrators. I had heard this 90% to 95% statistic many times, yet in my search for hard evidence of it, the West and Templer study was the only one I could find. This article was published in *Psychological Reports,* a journal that is not typically cited. However, because West and Templer reported statistics concerning the entire population of inmates convicted of child molestation in the state prison they examined, I felt that no one could argue the with the accuracy of the figure. I searched perhaps 200 national crime statistics charts, journal articles, and books to confirm this statistic, so its absence is further evidence to me of the covert nature of racism.

Incidentally, I have yet to hear any of my White friends, colleagues, or acquaintances say how offended they were when they passed a woman with a child who shielded her child from them.

☐ Conclusions

Although most of us would like to believe that we have put racism behind us, the modern forms of racism are subtle and insidious. It is in the air that we breathe. It does not matter if one is a brilliant psychologist, a hard-working news correspondent, or an average citizen who is being bombarded by these covert messages. It takes vigilance to detect these forms of racism and expose them for what they are—unfortunate and secretive ways of perpetuating racial stereotypes, biased attitudes, and discrimination. It is my firm belief that most people are of good will and that once they understand their own contribution to this perpetuation, they will work to purge it from their repertoire. However, this work is difficult, and we all need to help one another to identify and expose these subtle forms of racism.

☐ References

Abramson, L., Seligman, M. E. P., & Teasdale, J. D. (1978). Learned helplessness in humans: Critique and reformulation. *Journal of Abnormal Psychology, 87,* 49–74.

American Psychological Association. (1978). *Publication manual of the American Psychological Association* (3rd ed.). Washington, DC: Author.

Bernal, M. E., & Padilla, A. M. (1982). Status of minority curricula and training in clinical psychology. *American Psychologist, 37,* 780–787.

Campbell, D. T., & Stanley, J. C. (1963). *Experimental and quasi-experimental designs for research.* Chicago: Rand McNally.

Choney, S. K., Berryhill-Paapke, E., & Robbins, R. R. (1995). The acculturation of American Indians: Developing frameworks for research and practice. In J. G. Ponterotto, J. M. Casas, L. A. Suzuki, & C. M. Alexander (Eds.), *Handbook of multicultural counseling* (pp. 73–92). Thousand Oaks, CA: Sage.

Comas-Díaz, L. (1994). An integrative approach. In L. Comas-Díaz & B. Greene (Eds.), *Women of color: Integrating ethnic and gender identities in psychotherapy* (pp. 287–318). New York: Guilford.

Federal Bureau of Investigation. (1997). *Uniform reports for the United States 1996.* Washington, DC: Author.

Korchin, S. J. (1980). Clinical psychology and minority problems. *American Psychologist, 35,* 262–269.

Parham, T. A. (1990, August). Do the right thing: Racial discussion in counseling psychology. In J. G. Ponterotto (Chair), *The White American researcher in multicultural counseling: Significance and challenges.* Symposium presented at the 98th Annual Convention of the American Psychological Association, Boston.

Richardson, E. H. (1981). Cultural and historical perspectives in counseling American

Indians. In D. W. Sue (Ed.), *Counseling the culturally different: Theory and practice* (pp. 216–255). New York: Wiley.

Ridley, C. R. (1989). Racism in counseling as an adverse behavioral process. In P. B. Pedersen, J. G. Draguns, W. J. Lonner, & J. E. Trimble (Eds.), *Counseling across cultures* (3rd ed., pp. 55–77). Honolulu: University of Hawaii Press.

Ridley, C. R. (1995). *Overcoming unintentional racism in counseling and therapy: A practitioner's guide to intentional intervention.* Thousand Oaks, CA: Sage.

Rosewater, L. B. (1990). Diversifying feminist psychotherapy and practice: Broadening the concept of victimization. *Women and Therapy, 9,* 299–311.

Sartwell, C. (1998, June 21). White America needs its bigotry. *The Los Angeles Times,* M5.

Seligman, M. E. P. (1968). Chronic fear produced by unpredictable electric shock. *Journal of Comparative Physiological Psychology, 66,* 402–411.

Seligman, M. E. P. (1975). *Helplessness.* San Francisco: Freeman.

Seligman, M. E. P. (1991). *Learned optimism.* New York: Knopf.

Seligman, M. E. P. (1998). *Learned optimism* (2nd ed.). New York: Knopf.

Seligman, M. E. P., Rossellini, R. A., & Kozak, J. J. (1975). Learned helplessness in the rat: Time course, immunization, and reversibility. *Journal of Comparative Physiological Psychology, 88,* 542–547.

Sue, S. (1998, August). Asian American mental health: Research trends and directions. In G. Y. Iwamasa (Chair), *Multicultural mental health research—current status and future directions.* Symposium presented at the 106th annual convention of the American Psychological Association, San Francisco.

Sue, S. (1999, January). *Science, ethnicity and bias: Where have we gone wrong?* Keynote address presented at the National Multicultural Conference and Summit, Newport Beach, CA.

Sue, D. W., Carter, R. T., Casas, J. M., Fouad, N. A., Ivey, A. E., Jensen, M., LaFromboise, T., Manese, J. E., Ponterotto, J. G., & Vazquez-Nutall, E. (1998). *Multicultural counseling competencies: Individual and organizational development.* Thousand Oaks, CA: Sage.

Tatum, B. D. (1997). *"Why are all the Black kids sitting together in the cafeteria?" and other conversations about race.* New York: Basic Books.

West, J., & Templer, D. I. (1994). Child molestation, rape, and ethnicity. *Psychological Reports, 75,* 1326.

Disguised Racism
in the Broader Society

How do people get wrongfully convicted? Racial discrimination—among cops, prosecutors and jurors—can certainly be a factor. Clarence Brandley, an African-American janitor, was accused of killing a white girl in Texas in 1980. A police officer allegedly told Brandley and a white janitor that one of them would hang for the crime, then turned to Brandley and added, "Since you're the nigger, you're elected." It was later shown that prosecutors suppressed evidence; Brandley was freed after 10 years in prison.

John McCormick (November 9, 1998, p. 64, *Newsweek*)

Certainly, blatant racism, as depicted in the above story on the inequities of the criminal justice system, still exists. But as indicated in the previous chapter, such overt forms of racism are not the principal problem in modern society. Old, blatant forms of racism are readily rejected by most people, today; covert, subtle forms of racism are difficult to detect and are therefore given the weight of "logical" argument. Well-meaning, principled people can be taken in by logical-sounding positions, unaware of the racist roots underlying those positions. This chapter presents some observations by multicultural theorists of how subtle forms of racism are made palatable by intellectual-sounding arguments, some of which are even based on a sprinkling of scientific research.

☐ Modern Forms of Racism

Consider the following two possibilities: (1) Factors such as race, ethnicity, and gender should be taken into account when determining the most qualified person for a particular job; (2) The most qualified person for a particular job should be hired regardless of race, ethnicity, or gender. Which of these two alternatives do you support? If you are like most Americans, you favor no. 2. There seems to be a perception that people hired on the basis of affirmative action are less well qualified than their White male counterparts. However, this assumes that aspects of race, ethnicity, and gender fall outside of one's definition of "qualification" for positions. Those who have been engaging in modern or symbolic forms of racism have convinced most Americans that race, ethnicity, and gender should have nothing to do with job qualifications.

I engaged in a class discussion with a White woman in my undergraduate cross-cultural course on the topic of affirmative action. She said that her boyfriend had always wanted to become a police officer. She went along with him to take a qualification test. Although her boyfriend scored slightly higher on the test than she did, she was invited to train at the police academy and her boyfriend was not. She felt this was entirely unfair because she did not feel herself to be as qualified as he was. She said it was only the police academy's affirmative action policy of increasing the number of its Latino and female members that garnered her the invitation, so she refused it. The next time her boyfriend applied for a position and took the entrance examination, he passed and was invited to attend the academy.

I pointed out to her that there are many fewer women in the police force, and that in situations such as domestic violence and responding to rape victims, women officers are often needed. Thus, the very fact that women are women *should* play a role in determining whether applicants are qualified for particular positions. Certainly, had she scored below a certain grade, she would not be considered qualified to become an officer, but if she had scored above a particular level, her gender should be a consideration. The reason the police force wanted to increase the number of Latino officers was that Los Angeles County is so heavily populated by Latinos that it only made sense to seek Latino officers so that members of the community would feel comfortable with the members of their police force. Moreover, such officers would be much more likely to speak Spanish, which was a very important qualification. However, those engaging in symbolic racism have convinced most of America that "qualification" is measured only by test scores.

Jones (1997) identified three forms of modern racism that are based on negative attitudes that persist in those who otherwise believe themselves to be unprejudiced in racial matters. These forms of racism are symbolic racism, modern racism, and aversive racism.

Symbolic Racism

Symbolic racism is based upon Sears' (1988) notion that hostility toward Blacks (and, presumably, all people of color) still exists among many Whites, and that this hostility can be expressed in terms of adherence to the "traditional values" of individualism and the Protestant work ethic. According to Jones (1997) and Sears (1988), symbolic racism can be measured by the degree to which individuals support three basic notions: (1) antagonism toward Black demands, (2) resentment of gains made by Blacks through "special favors," and (3) denial of the continued existence of discrimination.

Sears and his colleagues (e.g., Kinder & Sears, 1981; Sears, 1988) were able to demonstrate that people's adherence to the above three basic notions of symbolic racism had predictive value in determining attitudes toward and voting behavior on racially charged issues, such as affirmative action, bilingual education, and voting for Black candidates. Moreover, symbolic racism has the advantage of protecting individuals from seeing themselves as being racist according to traditional definitions of racism, instead seeing themselves as holding traditional values. Jones (1997) wrote:

> Sears argues that symbolic racism has a far greater effect on white attitudes and behavior than does the old-fashioned, hostility–antagonism racial hatred. Symbolic racism is highly correlated with traditional racism in that both have a strong antiblack component. However, it is different in that it incorporates a focus on traditional values, whereas traditional racism does not. (p. 125)

Modern Racism

Jones (1997) identified McConahay (1986) as defining the term "modern racism." This form of racism holds that racism is a past problem, not a contemporary one, that those who are working toward the end of racism are pushing their agenda too hard, that the tactics of those working against racism are unfair, and that any gains achieved through these "unfair" tactics are fundamentally undeserved. This form of racism is related to symbolic racism, although people who can be characterized as modern racists consciously feel that racism is bad. These individuals, instead, see their own (prejudiced) views as being based on facts and believe that they do not hold what are traditionally thought to be racist views.

Jones (1997, pp. 126–127) reported that over the years, McConahay's (1986) Modern Racism Scale (MRS) has been distilled down to six items:

1. Over the past few years, the government and news media have shown more respect to Blacks than they deserve to be shown. (Strongly agree = 5)
2. It is easy to understand the anger of Black people in the United States. (Strongly disagree = 5)
3. Discrimination against Blacks is no longer a problem in the United States. (Strongly agree = 5)
4. Over the past few years, Blacks have received more economically than they deserve. (Strongly agree = 5)
5. Blacks are getting too demanding in their push for equal rights. (Strongly agree = 5)
6. Blacks should not push themselves where they are not wanted. (Strongly agree = 5)

The MRS has, according to Jones (1997), demonstrated its usefulness in measuring racial prejudice and has become an important tool in the racism literature.

Aversive Racism

Jones (1997) identified Gaertner and Dovidio (1986) as the proponents of aversive racism. This form of racism is not hostile or aggressive toward Blacks (and, presumably, other people of color) but is more avoidant. The avoidance is based on the idea that these individuals have been raised in a culture that promotes racism while also promoting egalitarian views. Thus, a conflict results. Because conflict is aversive, one can avoid the conflict by avoiding contact with Blacks (ethnic minorities).

Gaertner and Dovidio (1986) posited that whenever egalitarian norms are equivocal, aversive racists avoid contact with Blacks or do not assist Blacks as readily as they do when egalitarian norms are clear. Moreover, if there are possible nonracial factors that could allow the rationalization of unfavorable behaviors toward Blacks, aversive racists would seize upon these factors even under conditions of clear egalitarian norms. Their research supported these claims (e.g., Dovidio & Gaertner, 1981; Frey & Gaertner, 1986).

Overall, Jones (1997, p. 130) concludes that three factors underlie symbolic, modern, and aversive forms of racism:

1. Negative affect associations to Black people;
2. Ambivalence between feelings of nonprejudice or egalitarianism and those negative feelings;
3. A tendency for people who aspire to a positive, egalitarian self-image to nevertheless show racial biases when they are unaware of how to appear nonbiased.

As discussed in the last chapter, modern forms of racism are covert in nature and, as such, are insidious. They have measurable effects upon the conduct of individuals, yet racism can be denied because only the old-fashioned, traditional forms of racism are considered to be truly racist.

At my own university, we have an ethnic minority president whose two major goals are to promote diversity in the campus community and to modernize our technology base. In his 7 years as president, he has made large gains in both of these areas. For example, the university is located in a predominantly Hispanic/Latino and Asian area, but when he took over as president, the student population was predominantly White. Now the population is predominantly Hispanic/Latino and Asian. However, a substantial number of faculty members have opposed this president from the very beginning. Under general claims of wanting things to be "like they used to be," they have attempted to undermine his authority, taking actions that culminated in a call for a vote of no confidence to be sent to the chancellor of the university system. (Incidentally, none of them have claimed that they do not want their new computer systems, so one has to wonder what is meant by wanting things to be "like they used to be.")

Interestingly, this call for a vote of no confidence came a year after a previous attempt to do the same thing. Leaders of the Academic Senate attempted to get the entire senate to endorse this plan, and it was voted down by a substantial margin. A positive result of this confrontation was an agreement between the president and leaders of the senate to meet on a regular basis. Although there were still some disagreements, it seemed that the entire atmosphere had changed. However, near the end of academic year 1997–1998, when the president was out of town representing the university in Washington, DC, the leaders of the senate voted in executive session to go forward with this vote of no confidence. They sent out the ballots and an accompanying 14-page list of grievances against the president. Some of these grievances were legitimate, some were legitimate but had been resolved years before, and some were completely illegitimate. This 14-page list of grievances was so detailed, and its reproduction and the ballot preparation appeared so soon after the president's last meeting with the senate leadership and his subsequent departure for Washington, that one can only conclude that the leadership had been planning this vote regardless of how the meetings with the president were proceeding. Incidentally, although the Academic Senate represents the entire campus, the ballots were mailed only to professors on the campus, and only professors were allowed to vote on this issue.

Most of the ethnic minority faculty and other fair-minded individuals were appalled by this maneuver, and there was a concerted effort to let cooler heads prevail or at least to delay the vote until more information could be gathered. However, the leaders of the senate had called for the votes to be returned only 1 week after the ballots had been received and did not budge from this date. When one of the ethnic minority faculty members wondered out loud if there were some sort of underlying racial resistance that might be examined, she was immediately shouted down by numerous voices. This occurred despite the fact that (1) all of the ethnic minority organizations on campus were in strong support of the president, and (2) one of the president's main initiatives was to work for the diversification of the campus. There were other issues in the set of grievances, principally concerning the allocation of merit pay, and these issues allowed otherwise fair-minded individuals to cast their ballots in favor of the no confidence resolution. The resolution passed by a margin roughly equivalent to the percentage by which White faculty outnumber ethnic minority faculty on this campus. Modern forms of racism are insidious.

☐ Modern Forms of Racism in the Broader Society

The State of California

The state of California is often considered to be the bellwether of the nation. Its 1978 revolt against taxes set the stage for Ronald Reagan's election based on tax cuts in 1980; its years of electing conservative governors preceded the years of conservatism in the country. Although California is now swinging toward more liberal policies, its stance on race relations seems to portend continued resistance toward multiculturalism, as indicated by the passage of Propositions 187, 209, and 227.

In the autumn of 1994, Proposition 187, which cut social benefits to all illegal aliens, including children, was passed. It passed despite the fact that an unusual coalition of compassionate liberals and law-and-order policemen was formed to prevent its passage. The compassionate-liberal argument was that one should not deny social benefits such as health care to children who had no choice in their parents' decision to move to the United States. From a practical standpoint, poor health care would also lead to the spreading of disease to citizens and legal aliens. The law-and-order argument was that if illegal alien children were not allowed to attend school, they would be out in the streets and potentially become involved with the legal system. However, these arguments failed, and Proposition 187 passed by a wide margin.

Proposition 209, passed in 1996, eliminated affirmative action programs sponsored by the state, including college admission standards and state contracts to businesses. Despite the fact that the debate was framed to pit Asians and Whites against other ethnic minority groups, statistics indicate that Asians, along with other ethnic minority groups, voted against Proposition 209 (Duster, 1998). Arguments in favor of the passage of the proposition fell along the lines of the modern forms of racism: Blacks (and other ethnic minorities) are undeserving, affirmative action is unfair, and people should be admitted into higher education and get state contracts on their own merits. Interestingly, Proposition 209 specifically *denied* women and ethnic minorities any competitive advantage, but it *allowed* advantage based upon legacy (children of alumni receive special admissions consideration in higher education) and geographic area (individuals who are "less qualified" by objective measures but are from rural areas are given special consideration for both college admission and state contracting). Thus, the arguments calling for pure merit-based awards were disingenuous, as only gender and ethnic minority status were specifically denied special consideration.

Proposition 227 was passed in 1998. This proposition eliminated eligibility for bilingual education after 1 year, unless some overwhelming need was demonstrated by a school system. It was characterized as being supported by the Hispanic/Latino population—the population that would seem to benefit from the continuation of bilingual education—but exit polls taken on Election Day indicated that a majority of Hispanic/Latino voters actually opposed the measure.

A White majority bloc voted overwhelmingly for the passage of all three of the propositions. Even though ethnic minorities are now at or near majority status in California, well over 80% of the voters are White (Duster, 1998). Because the debates are framed along the lines of modern forms of racism, the racism remains undetected by most voters.

Because these forms of racism do not resemble old-fashioned forms of racism, direct reference to the racist nature of the propositions can lead to a backlash and an even greater adherence to the position of being against people of color. However, in all three of these cases, the trend of the public was toward voting these measures down (Duster, 1998). As people became more informed about the meaning of the issues they became more inclined to recognize the subtle racism behind them.

The Rest of the Nation

The issue of affirmative action is likely to be a major political debate for years to come. Conservative voices, couched in the language of modern forms of racism, have been opposing affirmative action for years (e.g., Belz, 1991; D'Souza, 1991; Nieli, 1991). Nieli (1991) has even warned that affirmative action will ultimately lead to civil war initiated by those who feel disadvantaged by affirmative action policies—that is, White males.

As evidenced by the passage of Proposition 209 and other national antiaffirmative action decisions, conservative voices are winning the battle at this time. White (1998) indicated that the disarray of the NAACP has allowed opponents of civil rights and affirmative action to take the initiative:

> Almost all efforts to increase minority participation in the workplace and on campus have been redefined by opponents as quotas and racial preferences. Lurid stories about white male job seekers or college applicants being passed over for less qualified blacks or women have been accepted as the norm, even though many of the tales turned out to be bogus. (p. 27)

However, White (1998) indicated that under the leadership of Julian Bond and Kwiesi Mfune, the NAACP has restored its focus and is ready to engage in the battle.

Still, conservative voices have proliferated in the past decade or two. Among the most vocal critics of affirmative action policies has been Dinesh D'Souza, who traveled the circuit of campuses and talk shows to promote his book attacking affirmative action policies (D'Souza, 1991). (Interestingly, Michael Kinsley, then cohost of the CNN show "Crossfire," wryly pointed out the irony of D'Souza's making a very good living by being paid to speak on college campuses where he rants about how voices like his are not being allowed to speak on college campuses.) According to D'Souza (1991), "Although university leaders speak of the self-evident virtues of diversity, it is not at all obvious why it is necessary to a first-rate education" (p. 230). He went on to write:

> The problem begins with a deep sense of embarrassment over the small number of minorities—blacks in particular—on campuses. University officials speak of themselves as more enlightened and progressive than the general population, so they feel guilty if the proportion of minorities at their institutions is smaller than in surrounding society. (p. 231)

D'Souza also attacked women and homosexuals as exploiting the race issue for their own "extremist" agenda.

Chang-Lin Tien, Chancellor of the University of California, Berkeley, and the first Asian Pacific American to be appointed to lead a major university in the United States, resigned over the 1996 University of California Regents' decision to eliminate affirmative action policies in the state's higher education system (he "officially" retired, although it was clearly in protest over the new policy). This occurred even before the passage of Proposition 209. Most of us in education noted that every single regent who was an educator voted to continue the state's affirmative action policy, but because the majority of the regents were noneducation appointees by Governor Pete Wilson, the policy was passed along strict ideological lines.

Tien (1995) indicated that diversifying a college campus—especially a public institution such as Berkeley—to the point where it at least somewhat reflects the diversity in the surrounding community is a basic charge, and to do anything less is to shun the citizens of the state. Moreover, he pointed out that as the campus became more diverse under his leadership, graduation rates increased concomitantly. Berkeley students have a 74% rate of graduation within 5 years, as compared to 48% in 5 years in the mid-1950s. Finally, in the freshman class admitted just before he wrote his article (autumn 1994), standards had been subjected to higher standards than the freshman class had been a decade earlier. The mean high school GPA for that class was 3.84, and the mean SAT score was 1225. "The numbers dispel the notion that diversity has somehow sacrificed the quality of our institution. In fact, the diversity has been coupled with rising standards" (Tien, 1995, p. 20).

As Tien (1995) implied, perhaps those who feel wronged by admission denial are misplacing their hostility. He stated that Berkeley received 22,700 applications for the autumn of 1995. Of these applications, 9,500 had a high school GPA of 4.0. Because of space limitations, only 3,470 students were to be admitted that fall, so even if one were to select students strictly on the basis of GPA, many students with perfect high school records would have to be denied admission. Quite clearly, something beyond numerical criteria had to be used to make final admissions decisions. Yet some of the students who were denied admission might point to ethnic minority students with slightly lower GPAs and blame them (and affirmative action policies) for their rejection.

Incidentally, I have been having affirmative action debates in my undergraduate courses in recent years. These debates are to culminate in term papers based on library research and each student's personal journey through the debate about affirmative action. The quarter typically begins with equal numbers of students for and against affirmative action, but those against affirmative action quickly discover that there is very little evidence in favor of the antiaffirmative action side of the equation, only opinions. They quickly discover that the overwhelming number of cases in this area are documented cases of discrimination against ethnic minorities and women; very few cases concern reverse discrimination. However, the reverse discrimination cases get most of the headlines and most of the attention in debates. Students typically find these affirmative action debates and their own processes of discovery to be valuable experiences. For example, one student who initially was firmly against affirmative action wrote in his term paper:

> I consider this debate an extremely valuable experience. This debate and personal research has given me the chance to undo all my earlier misunderstandings regarding affirmative action. Before I participated in this project, my personal belief was always against affirmative action. It is partially due to the many common myths and misleading arguments that I often hear from the media. Because of the complexity of this issue, I never had the time nor the chance to verify these misleading [pieces of] information. (Asian/Pacific male no. 1)

"Shock" Humor

Another way in which racist material is disseminated is through the guise of humor or intentionally provocative commentary. Protected by cries of free speech, some individuals gain notoriety by using the public airwaves to make subtly or not-so-subtly racist remarks. Many of these individuals have found "legitimate" outlets for espousing their ultraconservative ideology, from Rush Limbaugh and G. Gordon Liddy on talk radio to Patrick J. Buchanan and Robert Novak on television. However, although I disagree with their positions, I can see that there is reason behind their words and we can, at least potentially, engage in a thoughtful dialogue about the issue. What I feel is more damaging is the medium that allows so-called shock jocks to advocate racist positions under the guise of "entertainment" or shock value. One such shock jock is Doug Tracht.

Doug Tracht was a disc jockey for WARW, a rock station in the Washington, DC, area. He played a selection from African American hip-hop singer Lauryn Hill, who won a record-breaking five Grammy Awards in one year. After playing the selection, he commented, "No wonder people drag them behind trucks" ("D.C. 'Shock Jock,'" 1999). This was in reference to the terrible dragging death of James Byrd, Jr., in Jasper, Texas. Just prior to the time Tracht had made his remarks, the horrific details of the dragging death were being made public. These details included the length of time medical examiners estimated Byrd remained conscious, trying to keep his head off the pavement, the limbs strewn along the side of the road, and that ultimately, his head had been ripped off his torso. The timing of this comment was such that these sickening images were still in listeners' minds.

Although Tracht was fired from the radio station for this remark, many felt his firing came several years too late. A few years earlier, during the celebration of Martin Luther King, Jr., Day, Tracht had made a comment to the effect of, "If they kill four more of them, we can have a week off." Amazingly, WARW did not fire him at the time for making that insensitive remark, and he had a few more years to implant racist feelings in his listeners.

Matsuda (1993) addressed the question of why there tends not to be an outcry from those in nontargeted groups (typically the White majority) whenever individuals like Tracht make such blatantly racist remarks:

> The typical reaction of non-members is to consider the incidents isolated pranks, the product of sick but harmless minds. This is in part a defensive reaction: a refusal to believe that real people, people just like us, are racists. This disassociation leads logically to the claim that there is no institutional or state responsibility to respond to the incident. It is not that kind of real and pervasive threat that requires the state's power to quell. (p. 20)

The Bell Curve

The concept of intelligence—particularly genetically endowed intelligence—has been controversial for many years. Jensen (1969) took a firm position that intelligence is almost entirely heritable, and that measured differences among the races reflect fundamental genetic differences. Jensen took this stand despite the clear evidence that environmental factors greatly influenced measured intelligence. For example, Gottesman (1968) pointed out that identical twins raised apart show differences in measured intelligence that are greater than the differences between Whites and African Americans. Kagan (1969) concluded that environmental differences offer a much better explanation of variations in measured intelligence than does genetic makeup. In a related area—academic achievement—Sue and Okazaki (1990) stated that differences within racially identified groups far exceed differences among racially identified groups, so environmental factors must contribute much more to differences in academic achievement than do genetic factors.

The genetic argument resurfaced at the time of the publication of Herrnstein and Murray's (1994) *The Bell Curve: Intelligence and Class Structure in American Life*. Although Herrnstein had passed away by the time the book was published, Charles Murray participated in numerous interviews to promote his work. The book's conclusion—and Murray's pronouncements while on his book tour—was that there are genuine genetic differences in intelligence, and that society should be set up such that those with lower intelligence are at the service of those with higher intelligence. Sue and Sue (1999) concluded, "What is problematic about *The Bell Curve* is that it presents a good deal of genuine science sprinkled with science fiction and a political ideology aimed at creating an elite class in America" (p. 20).

Herrnstein and Murray defend themselves by stating that their book is not really about race but about social class. Moreover, even if one were to make assumptions about intelligence based upon racial group membership, this need not interfere with daily interactions among the races. However, they do not waver from their essential conclusions that true differences in measured intelligence exist. Jones (1997) critiqued Herrnstein and Murray's position:

> Gould (1994) notes *The Bell Curve*'s claim that cognitive ability ". . . almost always explains less than 20 percent of the variance . . . usually less than 10 percent and often less than 5 percent. What this means in English is that you cannot predict what a given person will do from his IQ score." Gould (1994) suggests that if you take the Herrnstein and Murray (1994) claim that about 60 percent of IQ differences can be explained by genetics, and given that these differences only explain about 5 to 20 percent of individual variation, then only 3 to 12 percent of variations among individuals can be accounted for by heritability! (This is based on 60% heritability × 5 to 20 percent of the variance explained.) What explains the other 88 to 97 percent? (p. 500)

Quite clearly, *The Bell Curve* opened up old wounds in the debate about the heritability of intelligence. However, what struck me about this entire debate was the readiness with which the public was willing to accept this book when Murray was on his book tour. It is indicative to me that such impulses are just barely under the surface in the general public and, to borrow from Sue and Sue (1999), how just a little science can make science fiction so palatable.

☐ Conclusions

Modern forms of racism are subtle and disguised. They are more often than not couched in terms that seem palatable to most well-intentioned individuals and have the effect of persuading such individuals of positions to which they might not normally give credence if they knew the root or intention of these arguments. Alternatively, they can be thought of as intentionally provocative and thus be discounted. Topics such as services to illegal aliens, affirmative action, bilingual education, and the subjugation of one class of individuals to another are couched in terms of economics, reverse discrimination, ineffective teaching and learning, and the heritability of intelligence, which gives these arguments an air of justice or science to back up their positions. However, when one examines these issues carefully, one sees the motivation behind them and the implications of such policies. More often than not, one rejects these positions upon closer inspection.

☐ References

Belz, H. (1991). *Equality transformed: A quarter-century of affirmative action.* New Brunswick, NJ: Transaction.

D.C. 'shock jock' fired after joke about dragging death. (1999, February 26). *Los Angeles Times*, p. A28.

Dovidio, J. F., & Gaertner, S. L. (1981). The effects of race, status, and ability on helping behavior. *Social Psychology Quarterly, 44,* 192–203.

D'Souza, D. (1991). *Illiberal education: The politics of race and sex on campus.* New York: Free Press.

Duster, T. (1998, February). Being White and being normal: Race as "relational" to both and "other" and resources. Paper presented at the . . . *then, what is "White"* conference, Riverside, CA.

Frey, D., & Gaertner, S. L. (1986). Helping and the avoidance of inappropriate interracial behavior: A strategy that can perpetuate a non-prejudiced self-image. *Journal of Personality and Social Psychology, 50,* 1083–1090.

Gaertner, S. L., & Dovidio, J. F. (1986). The aversive form of racism. In J. F. Dovidio & S. L. Gaertner (Eds.), *Prejudice, discrimination and racism* (pp. 61–90). Orlando, FL: Academic Press.

Gottesman, I. I. (1968). Biogenetics of race and class. In M. Deutsch, I. Katz, & A. R. Jensen (Eds.), *Social class, race, and psychological development.* New York: Holt, Rinehart, & Winston.

Gould, S. J. (1994, November 28). Curveball. *The New Yorker*, pp. 139–149.

Herrnstein, R. J., & Murray, C. (1994). *The bell curve: Intelligence and class structure in American life.* New York: Free Press.

Jensen, A. R. (1969). How much can we boost IQ and scholastic achievement? *Harvard Educational Review, 38,* 1–123.

Jones, J. M. (1997). *Prejudice and racism* (2nd ed.). New York: McGraw-Hill.

Kagan, J. S. (1969). Inadequate evidence and illogical conclusions. *Harvard Educational Review, 39,* 126–129.

Kinder, D. R., & Sears, D. O. (1981). Prejudice and politics: Symbolic racism versus racial threats to the good life. *Journal of Personality and Social Psychology, 40,* 414–431.

Matsuda, M. J. (1993). Public response to racist speech: Considering the victim's story. In M. J. Matsuda, C. R. Lawrence, III, R. Delgado, & K. W. Crenshaw (Eds.), *Words that wound: Critical race theory, assaultive speech, and the First Amendment.* Boulder, CO: Westview.

McConahay, J. B. (1986). Modern racism, ambivalence, and the Modern Racism Scale. In J. F. Dovidio & S. L. Gaertner (Eds.), *Prejudice, discrimination and racism* (pp. 91–126). Orlando, FL: Academic Press.

McCormick, J. (1998, November 9). The wrongly condemned: How many capital cases end up in false convictions? *Newsweek,* 64–66.

Nieli, R. (Ed.). (1991). *Racial preference and racial justice: The new affirmative action controversy.* Washington, DC: Ethics & Public Policy Center.

Sears, D. O. (1988). Symbolic racism. In P. A. Katz & D. A. Taylor (Eds.), *Eliminating racism: Profiles in controversy* (pp. 53–84). New York: Plenum.

Sue, D. W., & Sue, D. (1999). *Counseling the culturally different: Theory and practice* (3rd ed.). New York: Wiley.

Sue, S., & Okazaki, S. (1990). Asian-American educational achievements: A phenomenon in search of an explanation. *American Psychologist, 45,* 913–920.

Tien, C.-L. (1995). Affirming affirmative action. *Common ground: Perspectives on affirmative action and its impact on APAs.* Los Angeles: LEAP Asian Pacific American Public Policy Institute.

White, J. E. (1998, July 27). "It's still White supremacy": Julian Bond restores the focus of the N.A.A.C.P. *Time,* p. 27.

The Construction and Maintenance of Stereotypes

> My math professor told me I was lazy and did not try very hard in his class. I told him I was trying as hard as I could, but he didn't believe me. I came from a small village in rural Vietnam, and I did not have very much schooling before I came to America. But my professor said that all Asians were smart in math, so that must mean that I wasn't trying very hard in his class.
>
> Vietnamese student (personal communication, April 1986)

As the above story indicates, even what many consider to be positive stereotypes can be turned into straitjackets. Are all stereotypes bad, or can some be good? Are stereotypes inevitable by-products of human cognition, or can they be avoided? Although stereotypes were discussed briefly in Chapter 1, this chapter addresses the concept that stereotypes are constructions of mental processes.

☐ Definition of Stereotypes

Kenrick, Neuberg, and Cialdini (1999) defines "stereotyping" as "(t)he process of categorizing an individual as a member of a particular group and then inferring that he or she possesses the characteristics generally held by members of that group" (p. 414). Jones (1997) identified the literal root of the word "stereotype" and noted when this literal root was first applied to people:

Literally, a *stereotype* is a metal plate that is used to make duplicate pages of the same type. Social commentator Walter Lippman borrowed this term back in 1922 to describe what he considered to be a biased perception. The bias was evidenced by comparing those "pictures" we had in our heads of someone and the reality the person presented to us. The bias resulted from preconceptions that were the result of the stereotyping process, whereby we "stamped" every member of the group as a duplicate of every other member—in other words, we created a stereotype. When we encountered a member of the group, we did not see him or her realistically. Instead, we saw the image of him or her filtered through this mental picture of the group we had stereotyped. (p. 167)

As most in this area would agree, stereotypes are a cognitive component of human interactions; prejudice is the evaluative component, discrimination is the behavioral component, and racism is the institutionalized component. Some (e.g., Jones, 1997; Jussim, McCauley, & Lee, 1995) use the words "stereotype" and "prejudice" essentially interchangeably. Most of this book is focused upon eliminating or at least addressing discrimination and racism. An assumption upon which I am working is that most people are motivated to be less prejudiced than they are, but they need the awareness and the tools presented in this book to help themselves overcome these prejudices. Consequently, I am focusing upon stereotypes in this chapter because some literature suggests that stereotypes are natural products of cognitive processes.

☐ The Cognitive Miser Approach Versus the Social Reality Approach to Stereotypes

Ever since the so-called cognitive revolution influenced social psychology in the late 1970s and early 1980s, the focus of research on stereotypes has been on how stereotypes are an inevitable by-product of normal cognitive processes (e.g., Fiske & Taylor, 1984, 1991; Hamilton, 1981; Markus & Zajonc, 1985, Taylor, 1981; Wyer & Gordon, 1984). Essentially, this cognitive approach suggests that social information is quite complex, and in order to attend to as much information as possible, large pieces of information are collapsed into small, easily usable pieces of information. In collapsing large pieces of information into small, simplified pieces, we can free up other attentional resources to concentrate upon other important information. Cognitive psychologists call this "chunking." This approach has become known as the cognitive economy or cognitive miser approach to stereotypes.

According to the cognitive miser approach, when I enter a racially mixed room, if I can lump all racial and ethnic groups into separate categories, it would occupy only a few "bits" of my attentional resources. As Miller (1956) stated long ago, we can hold only seven or so bits of information in our minds at any one time, so a few bits of attentional resources can be used to attend to other information in the room. According to Miller, a bit can be as small as a single item or as large as an entire collection of items that can be represented in a single form. If all of our attentional resources were dedicated to finding out the complexity of even one person—much less a collection of outwardly appearing similar people—there would be no resources left to attend to anything else in the room. Thus, there is a cost/benefit exchange in which the cost of the perhaps slightly inaccurate information transmitted by the stereotype is offset by the range of information to which we can attend. This cognitive miser stance dominated research in stereotypes for nearly two decades.

More recently, many social psychologists have turned their attention to a social reality approach to stereotyping. This approach suggests that stereotypes reflect the social reality of various groups, conveying an essential truth about the groups (see Spears & Haslam, 1997, and Yzerbyt, Rocher, & Schadron, 1997, for reviews of this view). Spears and Haslam (1997) suggest that this approach has its roots in some of the seminal writings of the literature of stereotyping (e.g., Brunner, 1990; Lippman, 1922; Tajfel, 1969). Yzerbyt et al. (1997) discussed their position:

> In our view, stereotypes work as *enlightening gestalts;* they supply perceivers with extra information by building upon a rich set of interconnected pieces of data. Moreover, stereotypes comprise more than the list of attributes that help describe a particular social category. They also, and perhaps most importantly, include the underlying explanation that links these attributes together. (p. 21)

They based their view on the cognitive tradition of concept formation. Writers such as Rosch (1978) and Rosch and Mervis (1975), who borrowed their ideas from the philosopher Wittgenstein (1953), discussed how we form concepts based upon exemplars that represent different categories. Over time, we begin to abstract a prototype of the categories. This prototype becomes the basis upon which we make categorical judgments about new objects. This approach has been applied to successful investigations into person perception (e.g., Anderson & Klatzky, 1987; Brewer, 1988; Cantor & Mischel, 1977, 1979). If it can be applied successfully to individuals, why not to groups? Thus, if one were to encounter a number of individuals from various ethnic minority groups, one could abstract what one perceives to be the essence of each group, based upon exemplars of the groups.

From this concept formation/social reality perspective, Spears and Haslam (1997) empirically investigated the cognitive miser versus the social reality approaches. They found evidence in support of the social reality approach and concluded:

> For us the functionality of stereotyping lies in detecting [psychologically meaningful social] reality, not in saving cognitive energy. Following this view, we would thus argue that it is not the case, as is commonly supposed . . . that in a "perfect" world or given a longer life free from cognitive demands, people would always treat and perceive everyone else as individuals. For to do so would involve missing out on reality and effectively preclude social activities which necessarily rely upon group-based social categorical perception. . . ." (p. 206)

☐ Consensual Stereotypes

One aspect of the social reality approach to stereotypes is what Gardner (1994) calls the consensual stereotype view, also known as the socio-cultural approach (Ashmore & Del Boca, 1981). This view suggests that not only are stereotypes accurate and informative but they emerge from the group itself. This type of stereotype helps us to determine our own group norms. Moreover, Oakes, Haslam, and Turner (1994) suggested that such stereotypes are important in psychologically binding like-minded individuals together. This is the basis of social identity theory (e.g., Tajfel & Turner, 1986; Turner, 1975). According to Oakes et al. (1994), "People seek a *positive social identity*. Since the value of any group membership depends upon comparison with other relevant groups, positive social identity is achieved through the establishment of *positive distinctiveness* of the in-group from relevant out-groups" (p. 82). One of the negative results of this positive social identity is that it formed the basis for discrimination against out-group members.

For example, I may self-identify as a Democrat because my belief is that Democrats balance justice with freedom. This is a self-identification, and other like-minded individuals may identify themselves as Democrats for the same reasons I do. We all share this same view, and we also share the view that Republicans do not seek a balance between justice and freedom. Instead, Republicans place much more emphasis on issues of freedom, rather than justice. Because we both value freedom, the major difference between my conceptualizations of the two groups is that Democrats value justice more than Republicans do. Therefore, I emphasize this difference more when trying to convince others of the "correctness" of my political affiliation. I may also denigrate Republicans for not valuing justice, thus beginning my discrimination against Republicans.

☐ Negative Effects of Stereotyping

Regardless of whether stereotypes are unfortunate summaries of more complex constellations of behavior or accurate reflections of the essence of a group of individuals, the fact remains that stereotypes can be misused and can result in negative effects. The social reality perspective depends on a dispassionate, logically constructed development of one's conception of the target object. This is fine when attempting to categorize inanimate objects such as furniture or animals such as birds or mammals (see Rosch & Mervis, 1975), but as we know, the categorization of people is not a dispassionate exercise.

Motivation and Stereotypes

Hilton and von Hippel (1996) suggested that motivational factors play an important role in why, when, and how stereotypes occur. If a person is disliked, much more evidence is needed to convince the perceiver of the existence of a positive characteristic (intelligence) than a negative characteristic (lack of intelligence; see Ditto & Lopez, 1993). Similarly, if a person is liked, relatively little information is needed to reduce a negative stereotype (see Klein & Kunda, 1992, and Pedry & Macrae, 1994). Quite clearly, in a dispassionate, unmotivated state, all information should be weighed equally. Valence for or against the target object should not have any effect upon our categorization decisions.

Ascription of Stereotypes

To the extent that the dominant society gets to decide which characteristics or abilities are valued, the dominant group can also ascribe negative values to the characteristics shared by those in the nondominant position. Although not related to racial/ethnic stereotypes, a story I like to tell my students is one involving the value of different gender characteristics. I was on the Women's Studies Advisory Committee at Washington State University. One of the women reported that a male mathematics professor had said something like, "The reason women do not do well in mathematics is that mathematics is a very precise language, and women do not have the ability to think so precisely." Around this time, our campus was being visited by the president of Vladivostock University in Russia, a university that had a sister-university agreement with Washington State University. The president of that university said to our president something like, "I don't know what is wrong with women. They can only be mathematicians, doctors, and scientists. They do not seem to have the ability to write novels or poems." Clearly, those in power get to value their own characteristics and denigrate the characteristics of out-group members. Moreover, they seem to attribute this to some sort of essence of the out-group members as opposed to some sort of societal circumstance (see Pettigrew, 1979, on the "ultimate attribution error," also to be discussed later in this chapter).

Stereotypes as Filters

As discussed by Jones (1997), African Americans and other ethnic minorities commonly receive negative stereotype labels from the broader society. Often, it is these stereotypes that are relied upon rather than careful observation. Part of the problem with such imposition is that it allows the filtering in of only those pieces of evidence that confirm the stereotype, and it screens out those pieces of evidence that disconfirm the stereotype. Jones (1997) concluded that "stereotypic structures affect what we expect to happen in our social world when people who fit our stereotype appear. These expectations affect how we process social information, and what we remember about people" (p. 191).

Stereotypes Guiding Construal of Information

According to Jones (1997), stereotypes can also influence how information is construed or interpreted. As a demonstration of this, Darley and Gross (1983) led research participants to believe that a female child was from either a high or a low socioeconomic class. When the participants saw the child taking an examination and getting answers right and wrong, those who were led to think that she was from a high socioeconomic class believed that she got more answers correct than she actually did and believed the test to be harder than it actually was. The participants who were led to think that the child was from a lower socioeconomic class believed she got more answers incorrect and believed the test to be easier.

Stereotypes as Self-fulfilling Prophecies

Finally, Jones (1997) discussed how stereotypes can affect the actual behavior of the target of the stereotype. This is known as the self-fulfilling prophecy (e.g., Rosenthal & Jacobson, 1968). In an interesting demonstration of this phenomenon, Snyder, Tanke, and Berscheid (1977) led research participants to believe that they were interacting over the telephone with either an attractive or an unattractive partner. The partner did not know that the other participant had any knowledge about his or her attractiveness. The unsuspecting partners were videotaped and evaluated only visually (the sound was turned off). Judges rated the partners *thought* by the research participants to be attractive as being, in fact, more attractive; the partners thought to be unattractive were rated as being more unattractive. Again, these partners did not know that they were being labeled as attractive or unattractive, and the judges did not know anything about what was being said, what the partners or research participants knew or did not know, and so forth. However, the research partners elicited attractive or unattractive judgments in accordance with their preconceptions. In racial and ethnic stereotypes, if one held a stereotype that a certain ethnic minority had a tendency to be hostile, one might act defensive around a member of that ethnic minority group. This behavior might have a negative effect upon the stereotyped target (not quite explicitly but barely perceptibly), and his or her behavior might be more forceful in response to the defensiveness. This, in turn, causes more defensiveness, which then causes a more forceful response. In a very short time, both will be consciously aware of the forceful ("hostile") behavior of the target, thus confirming the initial stereotype.

Stereotype Threat

As noted in Chapter 1, Steele (1997) discussed the negative effects of what he termed "stereotype threat." Briefly, he found evidence that when African Americans were led to believe that their performance on a very difficult test would have some sort of diagnostic implications about the fundamental differences between Blacks and Whites in intelligence, their performance dropped. When there was no threat of confirming a negative stereotype, African American performance was equal to that of Whites. This was replicated in women who feared confirming the stereotype of the male/female differences in mathematical abilities in America. Again, when measured by performance under conditions in which the negative stereotype was not being confirmed, there were no differences between the two groups under investigation. However, differences became apparent when performance was linked to the negative stereotypes. This occurred even when this connection was very subtly implied.

One of the main problems with negative stereotypes (or with stereotypes in general) is that they are quite difficult to eliminate. As was discovered in the old series of studies investigating the autokinetic phenomenon (e.g., Jacobs & Campbell, 1961; Sherif, 1937), several generations of research participants had to pass through before the influence of one confederate was washed away. If it took several generations of participants to overcome something as dispassionate as a judgment involving the distance a pinpoint of light in a dark room has moved, imagine how many generations it will take to counteract years and years of emotionally charged opinions about different races! After an exhaustive examination of stereotypes, Hilton and von Hippel's (1996) first major conclusion was that we know more about how stereotypes are formed than we know about how to eliminate them.

☐ Attributions and Attributional Errors

As every social psychologist knows, the simplest form of attribution theory is a two-by-two matrix, with one of the dimensions being internal versus external attributions and the other dimension being stable versus unstable attributions. Thus, the attribution of a behavior could be the result of an internal and stable reason, an internal and unstable reason, and external and stable reason, or an external and unstable reason (e.g., Heider, 1958; Jones, Kanouse, Kelley, Nisbett, Valins, & Weiner, 1972; Kelley, 1967; Weiner, 1974, 1986). As Jones and Davis (1965) have pointed out, actors have a tendency to attribute their behaviors to external or unstable factors, whereas observers tend to attribute actors' behaviors to internal and stable factors. Thus, if I were to trip, I might attribute my stumble to the crack in the sidewalk, whereas you might attribute my stumble to my clumsiness.

Many social psychologists think the tendency to attribute the behaviors of someone else to internal or dispositional traits derives from the fact that many people are naive personality psychologists. If someone has behaved in a particular manner, it must be due to some deep-seated personality characteristic in the person. Ross (1977) has labeled this tendency to act like a personality psychologist the "fundamental attribution error." Aronson, Wilson, and Akert (1997) define the fundamental attribution error as "the tendency to overestimate the extent to which people's behavior is due to internal, dispositional factors and to underestimate the role of situational factors" (p. 126). Social psychologists would much more readily try to find the social or contextual factors that led to the particular behavior.

What if a person seeing me trip on a crack in the sidewalk were not only to attribute it to an internal, stable characteristic (my being clumsy) but also to generalize this trait to all Asians? The attribution would then be, "Gosh, I guess *all* Asians are clumsy! That's why Jeff tripped." If the person were to make this attribution, Pettigrew (1979) would call it the "ultimate attribution error." Aronson et al. (1997) defined the ultimate attribution error as "our tendency to make dispositional attributions about an entire group of people" (p. 498). They discussed how this process of making an ultimate attribution error was applied to the stereotype of Jews' being interested only in money:

> When the Jews were first forced to flee their homeland during the third Diaspora, some 2,500 years ago, they were not allowed to own land or become artisans in the new regions in which they settled. Needing a livelihood, some took to lending money—a profession they were allowed to have. Although this choice of occupation was an accidental byproduct of restrictive laws, it led to a dispositional attribution about Jews: that they were interested only in dealing with money and not in honest work, like farming. As this attribution became an ultimate error, Jews were labeled conniving, vicious parasites. . . . This dispositional stereotype contributed greatly to the barbarous consequences of anti-Semitism in Europe during the 1930s and 1940s and has persisted even in the face of clear, disconfirming evidence—such as that produced by the birth of the State of Israel, where Jews tilled the soil and made the desert bloom. (p. 498)

Deaux and her colleagues (e.g., Deaux, 1976, 1984; Deaux & Emswiller, 1974; Deaux & Farris, 1977; Deaux & Lewis, 1984, Deaux & Major, 1987; Deaux, Winton, Crowley, & Lewis, 1985) have proposed a gender expectancy model to explain the differences in attributions seen between men and women for successful and unsuccessful performance of various tasks. This model was developed to address the gender differences often observed, in which males tend to attribute successes to internal, stable factors and failures to external or unstable factors, whereas females tend to attribute successes to external or unstable factors and failures to internal, stable factors. Interestingly, this pattern of attribution has been found in those who have average to above-average self-esteem and in those who have below-average self-esteem, with the male pattern of attribution being similar to those with high self-esteem and the female pattern of attribution being similar to those with low self-esteem (Deaux, 1984).

Do men generally have high self-esteem and women generally have low self-esteem? Deaux says no. Rather, the differences are related to the fact that researchers often use tasks stereotypically associated with males (e.g., mathematics exercises). According to Deaux's gender expectancy model, because the task is consistent with the stereotype for males (males are supposed to do well in mathematics tasks), men would attribute their successes to high ability and their failures to bad luck, poor effort, or the difficulty of the task. On the other hand, because the task is inconsistent with the stereotype for females (females are supposed to do poorly in mathematics tasks), women would attribute their successes to luck, good effort, or the ease of the task and their failures to poor ability. However, if the task were a stereotypic female task such as supportive verbalizations, exactly the opposite attributional pattern would be the result. Thus, the attributional pattern found in past studies was a function more of an artifact of measurement than of true gender differences. I recall an anecdote told by Shelley Taylor (either in print or at an APA convention) about a student who looked at her vita and commented, "Wow, you must work very hard!" To offer the student an alternative explanation, Taylor said, "No, not especially. I'm just smart."

In a similar vein, if a negative stereotype is ascribed to an ethnic minority group and a member of that group were to behave in a manner consistent with the stereotype, the stereotype would be reinforced. However, if a member were to behave in a manner inconsistent with the stereotype, the behavior could be attributed to some sort of situational factor. I recall that when the riots in Los Angeles occurred after the first Rodney King trial decision was announced, people tended to feel that the riots simply reinforced people's notion that African Americans were violent. This was brought into sharp focus when videotapes of the Reginald Denny beating were replayed over and over. However, people tended not to attribute care to the African Americans who pulled Reginald Denny to safety.

☐ The Media and the Maintenance of Stereotypes

As implied in the last paragraph, the media can have a major effect upon the formation and maintenance of stereotypes. Many would contend that the contributions of the media are crucial in this matter (e.g., Feng, 1995; Jones, 1997; Mok, 1998; Paik, 1971; Ponterotto & Pedersen, 1993; Williams, LaRose, & Frost, 1981). Perhaps the stereotype of African Americans' being violent was maintained after the Rodney King riots because the Reginald Denny beating was replayed much more often than was his rescue.

As I discussed in Chapter 2, when we discuss the media and stereo-type maintenance in my multicultural courses, I point out to students how the media refer to inner-city violence as Black-on-Black violence. However, when the media refer to violence in the suburbs or other forms of violence involving White communities, they never call them White-on-White violence.

This last point was sadly and poignantly brought home by an editorial by Courtland Milloy (1999). He was writing about the horrible tragedy at Columbine High School in Littleton, Colorado, where two White males who were members of a group of students known as the Trench Coat Mafia killed and wounded dozens of their classmates in a planned assault on the school. Bombs and boobie traps were also set all over the school. Milloy discussed how there exists a "parallel universe" for Blacks and Whites in this country. In this parallel universe, perspectives of the same events were quite different. He said:

> In my parallel world, you hear comments like, "I'm so glad those killers weren't Black. You know we'd all be in trouble if they were." . . . In the parallel universe, there is acute awareness that White America responds differently when killers are Black and that its police apparatus can easily become a Gestapo-like operation. . . . In Columbine, the parents of the killers were not questioned by police for several hours after the crimes, even though police knew that bombs had been made in their homes. Had the killers been Black, the parents would no doubt have been hauled off in handcuffs in front of television cameras, and everybody who knew them would be under suspicion. . . . In Columbine, a TV reporter actually referred to one of the killers as "a gentleman who drove a BMW." The shooters also were referred to as members of a "clique," not a gang, and they were—we were reminded again and again—so full of academic promise. This obvious identification with the killers, and the reluctance to demonize them as Blacks would have been, did not go over well in the parallel universe.

Milloy went on to discuss the differential treatment by politicians and the media of violence in the inner city and in the suburbs. When violence occurs in the inner city, discussions of crackdowns on hoodlums arise. When violence occurs in the suburbs, discussions arise about how society is to blame because of the culture of violence portrayed in the media and the availability of guns.

☐ Conclusions

Many believe that stereotypes are natural results of our desire to categorize large pieces of information. This categorization helps us to save attentional resources for other forms of information that require our attention. However, social stereotypes are not necessarily benignly constructed. Portrayals in the media can profoundly bias our formation of opinions of groups other than our own. Is there any solution to this problem of media portrayal? I do not know. However, I believe that we all must be aware of these discrepancies and make our students aware of them. At some point, public action must take place, and if those who control the media are made aware of their bias by enough people, change can occur.

 # References

Anderson, S. M., & Klatzky, R. L. (1987). Traits and social stereotypes: Levels of categorization in person perception. *Journal of Personality and Social Psychology, 53,* 235–246.

Aronson, E., Wilson, T. D., & Akert, R. M. (1997). *Social psychology* (2nd ed.). New York: Longman.

Ashmore, R. D., & Del Boca, F. K. (1981). Conceptual approaches to stereotypes and stereotyping. In D. L. Hamilton (Ed.), *Cognitive processes in stereotyping and intergroup behavior* (pp. 1–35). Hillsdale, NJ: Erlbaum.

Brewer, M. B. (1988). A dual process model of impression formation. In T. K. Srull & R. S. Wyer (Eds.), *Advances in social cognition* (Vol. 1, pp. 1–36). Hillsdale, NJ: Erlbaum.

Brunner, J. S. (1990). *Acts of meaning.* Cambridge, MA: Harvard University Press.

Cantor, N., & Mischel, W. (1977). Traits as prototypes: Effects on recognition memory. *Journal of Personality and Social Psychology, 35,* 38–48.

Cantor, N., & Mischel, W. (1979). Prototypes in person perception. In L. Berkowitz (Ed.), *Advances in experimental social psychology* (Vol. 12, pp. 3–52). New York: Academic Press.

Darley, J. M., & Gross, P. H. (1983). A hypothesis-confirming bias in labeling effects. *Journal of Personality and Social Psychology, 44,* 20–33.

Deaux, K. (1976). Sex: A perspective on the attribution process. In J. H. Harvey, W. J. Ickes, & R. F. Kidd (Eds.), *New directions in attribution research* (Vol. 1, pp. 335–352). Hillsdale, NJ: Erlbaum.

Deaux, K. (1984). From individual differences to social categories: Analysis of a decade's research on gender. *American Psychologist, 39,* 105–116.

Deaux, K., & Emswiller, E. (1974). Explanations of successful performance on sex-linked tasks: What is skill for the male is luck for the female. *Journal of Personality and Social Psychology, 29,* 80–85.

Deaux, K., & Farris, E. (1977). Attributing causes for one's own performance: The effects of sex, norms, and outcome. *Journal of Research in Personality, 11,* 59–72.

Deaux, K., & Lewis, L. L. (1984). The structure of gender stereotypes: Interrelationships among components and gender label. *Journal of Personality and Social Psychology, 46,* 991–1004.

Deaux, K., & Major, B. (1987). Putting gender into context: An interactive model of gender-related behavior. *Psychological Review, 94,* 369–389.

Ditto, P. H., & Lopez, D. A. (1993). Motivated skepticism: Use of differential decision criteria for preferred and nonpreferred conclusions. *Journal of Personality and Social Psychology, 63,* 568–584.

Feng, P. (1995). In search of Asian American cinema. *Cineaste, 21,* 32–36.

Fiske, S. T., & Taylor, S. E. (1984). *Social cognition*. Reading, MA: Addison-Wesley.

Fiske, S. T., & Taylor, S. E. (1991). *Social cognition* (2nd ed.). New York: McGraw-Hill.

Gardner, R. C. (1994). Stereotypes as consensual beliefs. In M. P. Zanna & J. M. Olson (Eds.), *The psychology of prejudice: The Ontario symposium* (Vol. 7, pp. 1–27). Hillsdale, NJ: Erlbaum.

Hamilton, D. L. (1981). Stereotyping and intergroup behavior: Some thoughts on the cognitive approach. In D. L. Hamilton (Ed.), *Cognitive processes in stereotyping and intergroup behavior* (pp. 333–353). Hillsdale, NJ: Erlbaum.

Heider, F. (1958). *The psychology of interpersonal relations*. New York: Wiley.

Hilton, J. L., & von Hippel, W. (1996). Stereotypes. In J. T. Spence, J. M. Darley, & D. J. Foss (Eds.), *Annual review of psychology* (Vol. 47, pp. 237–271). Palo Alto, CA: Annual Reviews.

Jacobs, R. C., & Campbell, D. T. (1961). The perpetuation of an arbitrary tradition through several generations of a laboratory microculture. *Journal of Abnormal and Social Psychology, 62*, 649–658.

Jones, E. E., & Davis, K. E. (1965). From acts to dispositions: The attribution process in social psychology. In L. Berkowitz (Ed.), *Advances in experimental social psychology* (Vol. 2, pp. 219–266). New York: Academic Press.

Jones, E. E., Kanouse, D. E., Kelley, H. H., Nisbett, R. E., Valins, S., & Weiner, B. (Eds.). (1972). *Attribution: Perceiving the causes of behavior*. Morristown, NJ: General Learning Press.

Jones, J. M. (1997). *Prejudice and racism* (2nd ed.). New York: McGraw-Hill.

Jussim, L. J., McCauley, C. R., & Lee, Y.-T. (1995). Why study stereotype accuracy and inaccuracy? In Y.-T. Lee, L. J. Jussim, & C. R. McCauley (Eds.), *Stereotype accuracy: Toward appreciating group differences* (pp. 3–28). Washington, DC: American Psychological Association.

Kelley, H. H. (1967). Attribution theory in social psychology. In D. Levine (Ed.), *Nebraska symposium on motivation* (Vol. 15, pp. 192–238). Lincoln, NE: University of Nebraska Press.

Kenrick, D. T., Neuberg, S. L., & Cialdini, R. B. (1999). *Social psychology: Unraveling the mystery*. Boston: Allyn & Bacon.

Klein, W. M., & Kunda, Z. (1992). Motivated person perception: Constructing justifications for desired beliefs. *Journal of Experimental Social Psychology, 28*, 145–168.

Lippman, W. (1922). *Public opinion*. New York: Harcourt, Brace and World.

Markus, H., & Zajonc, R. (1985). The cognitive perspective in social psychology. In G. Lindzey & E. Aronson (Eds.), *Handbook of social psychology* (Vol. 1, pp. 137–230). New York: Random House.

Miller, G. A. (1956). The magical number seven, plus or minus two: Some limits on our capacity for processing information. *Psychological Review, 63*, 81–97.

Milloy, C. (1999, May 2). A look at tragedy in Black, White. *Washington Post*, p. C1.

Mok, T. A. (1998). Getting the message: Media images and stereotypes and their effect on Asian Americans. *Cultural Diversity and Mental Health, 4*, 185–202.

Oakes, P. J., Haslam, S. A., & Turner, J. S. (1994). *Stereotyping and social reality*. Oxford: Blackwell.

Paik, I. (1971). That Oriental feeling: A look at the caricatures of the Asians as sketched by American movies. In A. Tachiki, E. Wong, & F. Odo (Eds.), *Roots: An Asian American reader* (pp. 30–36). Los Angeles: Continental Graphics.

Pedry, L. F., & Macrae, C. N. (1994). Stereotypes and mental life: The case of the motivated but thwarted tactician. *Journal of Experimental Social Psychology, 30*, 303–325.

Pettigrew, T. F. (1979). The ultimate attribution error: Extending Allport's cognitive analysis of prejudice. *Personality and Social Psychology Bulletin, 5*, 461–476.

Ponterotto, J. G., & Pedersen, P. B. (1993). *Preventing prejudice*. Newbury Park, CA: Sage.

Rosch, E. (1978). Principles of categorization. In E. Rosch & B. Lloyd (Eds.), *Cognition and categorization* (pp. 28–49). Hillsdale, NJ: Erlbaum.

Rosch, E., & Mervis, C. B. (1975). Family resemblances: Studies in the internal structure of categories. *Cognitive Psychology, 7,* 573–605.

Rosenthal, R., & Jacobson, L. F. (1968). Teacher expectations for the disadvantaged. *Scientific American, 218* (#4), 19–23.

Ross, L. (1977). The intuitive psychologist and his shortcomings: Distortions in the attribution process. In L. Berkowitz (Ed.), *Advances in experimental social psychology* (Vol. 10, pp. 173–220). Orlando, FL: Academic Press.

Sherif, M. (1937). An experimental approach to the study of attitudes. *Sociometry, 1,* 90–98.

Snyder, M., Tanke, E. D., & Berscheid, E. (1977). Social perception and interpersonal behavior: On the self-fulfilling nature of social stereotypes. *Journal of Personality and Social Psychology, 35,* 656–666.

Spears, R., & Haslam, S. A. (1997). Stereotyping and the burden of cognitive load. In R. Spears, P. J. Oakes, N. Ellemers, & S. A. Haslam (Eds.), *The social psychology of stereotyping and group life* (pp. 171–207). Oxford: Blackwell.

Steele, C. M. (1997). A threat in the air: How stereotypes shape intellectual identity and performance. *American Psychologist, 52,* 613–629.

Tajfel, H. (1969). Cognitive aspects of prejudice. *Journal of Social Issues, 25,* 79–97.

Tajfel, H., & Turner, J. C. (1986). The social identity theory of intergroup behaviour. In S. Worschel & W. G. Austin (Eds.), *Psychology of intergroup relations* (2nd ed., pp. 7–24). Chicago: Nelson-Hall.

Taylor, S. E. (1981). A categorization approach to stereotyping. In D. L. Hamilton (Ed.), *Cognitive processes in stereotyping and intergroup behavior* (pp. 83–114). Hillsdale, NJ: Erlbaum.

Turner, J. C. (1975). Social comparison and social identity: Some prospects for intergroup behaviour. *European Journal of Social Psychology, 5,* 149–178.

Weiner, B. (1974). *Achievement motivation and attribution theory*. Morristown, NJ: General Learning Press.

Weiner, B. (1986). *An attribution theory of emotion and motivation*. New York: Springer-Verlag.

Williams, F., LaRose, R., & Frost, F. (1981). *Children, television, and sex-role stereotyping*. New York: Praeger.

Wittgenstein, L. (1953). *Philosophical investigations*. New York: Macmillan.

Wyer, R. S., Jr., & Gordon, S. E. (1984). The cognitive representation of social information. In R. S. Wyer, Jr., & T. K. Srull (Eds.), *Handbook of social cognition* (Vol. 2, pp. 73–150). Hillsdale, NJ: Erlbaum.

Yzerbyt, V., Rocher, S., & Schadron, G. (1997). Stereotypes as explanations: A subjective essentialistic view of group perception. In R. Spears, P. J. Oakes, N. Ellemers, & S. A. Haslam (Eds.), *The social psychology of stereotyping and group life* (pp. 20–50). Oxford: Blackwell.

CHAPTER

5

Laurie A. Roades
and Jeffery Scott Mio

Allies: How Are They Created and What Are Their Experiences?

In addressing resistance to important social issues, such as the acceptance of multiculturalism, feminism, lesbians and gay men, various religions, and so forth, we have found that such work is difficult to accomplish without the help of individuals who leave their own demographic group to help those being oppressed. These individuals are known as allies. In this chapter, we focus on an examination of the motivations of these allies and on experiences as allies. In so doing, we hope to reach a better understanding of allies and thus make a step toward setting up an environment conducive to the creation of more allies.

There have been allies throughout history—people who work on behalf of others and who take up unpopular causes, people who work on behalf of groups other than their own. There were Whites in the abolition movement who opposed U.S. slavery and worked toward its demise. Christians hid Jews in Europe during World War II, often risking their own lives in the process. Men have marched on behalf of equal rights for women, and heterosexuals continue to support the rights of lesbians and gay men not to be discriminated against in public or private life.

It is expected, and perhaps assumed, that members of minority or oppressed groups are interested in issues and causes related to their own experiences. For example, one would not be surprised to find gay men and lesbians working toward equal rights, Jews working to decrease anti-Semitism, or Asian Americans working to diminish racism prejudice, and discrimination. In fact, quite the opposite is probably true. Without knowing an individual personally, one would be likely to expect that an African American would be interested in and would work toward equal rights for African Americans and that a woman would be the first to speak up if an incidence of sexism arose. We are often surprised, however, to hear someone not a member of these specific groups address these issues publicly or be committed to work on their behalf. Why would a heterosexual man or woman march in a gay pride parade, or someone without any physical disabilities work to change laws to allow increased access for people who are physically challenged? These questions are somewhat more challenging to answer.

Allies are crucial as we work toward social justice and equality for all groups. Members of oppressed groups are usually in the minority (numerically or in terms of power), and they are often seen as having a biased, self-serving interest in the issues they address. Allies, in contrast, are often in a position to raise issues with members of their own respective dominant groups and often wield the power from which they benefit.

Beverly Tatum (1997) described the effectiveness of having a White ally come into her classes on multicultural issues to discuss racial issues:

> My White students, who often comment about how depressing it is to study racism, typically say that the opportunity to talk with this ally gave them renewed hope. Through her example, they see that the role of the ally is not to help victims of racism, but to speak up against systems of oppression and to challenge other Whites to do the same. (p. 109)

Therefore, it is important to understand more about how people become allies of groups other than their own and to examine what their experiences as allies are like.

What are allies? There is little published empirical research on the subject of allies in everyday life. Therefore, we have begun to conduct a new line of research in this area. In order to learn about the experience of being an ally from allies themselves, we identified individuals we know who serve as allies of various groups and asked them about their personal experiences as allies. All allies completed open-ended questionnaires that asked a series of questions about how they would define the term "ally," how they became allies, and what their experiences as allies have been like. Although our work is still preliminary in nature, these responses have allowed us to examine some central questions and identify some key themes of the experience of being an ally. We discuss some of these key themes and provide examples from our respondents' experiences as we try to understand how people choose to become allies and how their lives are affected by that decision.

☐ Definition of an Ally

Paul Kivel (1996), in his book *Uprooting Racism: How White People Can Work for Racial Justice,* emphasizes the importance of Whites' being allies of people of color, but states that "there is no one correct way to be an ally. Each of us is different" (p. 86). This leaves us, then, with the question of what exactly an ally is and what exactly it is that allies do. We asked allies we know to indicate how they would define an ally. Their responses were quite varied and no two were identical. However, allies identified several key elements they thought made someone an ally. These key elements include (1) recognition of the oppression experienced by groups other than one's own; (2) recognition of the privilege that comes with membership in a dominant group; and (3) active support of and effort to speak out for and stand up for others and work to change the status quo.

Some examples of their definitions of ally follow.

Someone who advocates for the rights of stigmatized or historically oppressed groups/peoples. (White, female, lesbian no. 1)

I think an ally is someone who is not a member of a particular oppressed group, but identifies with that group. This means being willing to take risks to stand up when that group is being oppressed. This could mean attending protests, signing petitions, or simply confronting people when homophobic, racist, or sexist comments are made. (African American, female, heterosexual no. 2)

I see an ally as someone who understands the relationship of privilege and oppression in society. An ally recognizes the privilege he/she has as a result of his/her power in society over an oppressed group. An ally works to use this power as an advocate for social change. An ally is an educator about how stereotypes and prejudice affect the oppressed group and what one can do to change. (Asian/Pacific American, male, heterosexual)

A person who actively works either to uncover, correct, or assist people with understanding power and privilege individuals or groups of people in this society have over other individuals or groups of people in this society. (White, male, heterosexual no. 2)

As you can see, recognition of issues related to privilege and oppression as well as active support of those who are oppressed are defining elements of being an ally. This is consistent with McIntosh's (1988) recognition of her own privileges and how these privileges give her an unearned advantage. However, many groups are oppressed or have minority status in this country. For which groups do allies see themselves advocating?

Most allies seem to serve as allies of two or more groups. Most commonly, White respondents identified persons of color, heterosexuals identified lesbians and gay men, and men identified women as groups for whom they saw themselves as allies. A number of respondents also identified persons disadvantaged as a result of social class and persons with disabilities. Groups less frequently cited as allied with, but still identified by at least one respondent, include people with HIV, students, Jews and other non-Christians, the elderly, and immigrants.

These findings suggest that being an ally is not something one does simply for one specific group. Rather, individuals who serve as allies tend to recognize privilege and oppression across at least some groups and actively work to provide support and make changes in several arenas. Whether this awareness and commitment to multiple groups developed simultaneously or sequentially is an area that still needs examination.

One question that remains is whether a person can serve as an ally only of groups different from one's own or if one can serve as an ally within one's own group. For example, one White lesbian identified herself as an ally of gays and lesbians, and one White, heterosexual male reported serving as an ally of other White, heterosexual males who are trying to decrease prejudice and discrimination through their own allied behavior. Are these true examples of allied behaviors? Can one be seen as an ally when working for causes that might benefit one's own group, or does being an ally require that one not benefit directly? It is possible that although a gay man or lesbian would obviously benefit from activism and the support of gay and lesbian activities, being a public advocate of such issues when it is possible to be invisible may be a form of allied behavior. This question requires further study. However, our guess is that within the group, these individuals are seen as allies, but that external observers—those in the position of power—may view these individuals as merely furthering their self-interested causes.

☐ **Why Do People Become Allies?**

Allies reported a number of different reasons, and often several reasons, for becoming involved with issues and serving as allies. In general, these responses fall into five primary categories: a sense of working toward justice, personal membership in an oppressed group, childhood up-bringing, religious and spiritual influences, and personal relationships with members of oppressed groups.

Justice Concerns

Many allies reported an awareness of their own personal privilege and recognition of the inequalities that often exist among groups in our society as the motivation for becoming allies. This understanding was often accompanied by a sense of moral outrage when they viewed prejudice and discrimination against others. Thus, allies viewed their allied behavior as being an important way they could help work to-ward creating a more just world.

> I think it was realizing that people I truly care about experience deep pain and struggle from . . . oppression. This realization initially made me experience a tremendous amount of guilt because I usually had the privilege. But then I grew toward realizing that I could do something about it. One way was through being an ally. (White, male, hetero-sexual no. 2)
>
> As a child, I was always shocked, indignant, outraged when someone was treated unfairly. (White, female, lesbian no. 1)
>
> . . . to build a coalition for social justice. We will never attain that within the current system but it is crucial that we never give up the struggle. (White, male, heterosexual no. 4)

Thus, allies had the sense that what they were doing was proper and "right." One African American, heterosexual, female ally simply re-ported that she became an ally "because it's the *right* thing to do, and it's something I *want* to do."

Personal Membership in an Oppressed Group

A second explanation for becoming an ally centers around being a member of an oppressed group and thus having an increased aware-ness of issues related to prejudice and discrimination. This sensitivity to the impact of bias and a commitment to equality can lead to becoming active in working for the rights of other groups.

> As a person of color, issues of racism and oppression were things I was struggling to make sense out of. In dealing with these issues, I was also learning about the various ways I had privilege and power in society. On a basic level, it became a matter of "do unto others. . . ." I learned that the things I wanted from the White community, as well as other communities of color, to help fight racism were the same things other oppressed groups needed of me. (Asian/Pacific American, male, heterosexual)

> My position as a minority has provided me with insight with regards to the many challenges faced by individuals who are outside the majority culture. . . . I wanted to provide similar support to my community and as an ally in communities different from my own. (White, female, lesbian no. 3)

Therefore, personal oppression has allowed these individuals to become more sensitive to individuals oppressed for other reasons.

Childhood Upbringing

For many allies, their childhood upbringing emphasized issues of equality and working toward social justice. Either their parents were active themselves or they encouraged their children to be active when they were young. Parental example guided them toward an awareness of inequality and the importance of fighting prejudice and discrimination.

> Egalitarian values were instilled in me by my parents who strongly identified as liberal Democrats who cared about civil rights and educational opportunity. (White, female, lesbian no. 2)

> . . . when I was young my parents seemed to be proud of my reaction to injustice. (White, female, lesbian no. 1)

> Mother had friends and views that did not support automatic cliquishness. Direct lessons not to discriminate against homo- and bisexual persons—it was irrational. (Asian/Pacific American, female, heterosexual)

Therefore, whether it was by example or intentional teaching, parents were instrumental in teaching allied behaviors.

Religious and Spiritual Influences

Some respondents reported that spiritual and religious beliefs motivated them to become active as allies. For some allies this included formal religious involvement, whereas for others it was more of a personal sense of spirituality. For example, one White, bisexual female reported that her "spiritual awakening as a Buddhist and Unitarian" influenced her to become an ally. Two other respondents reported a more general sense of spirituality. For example, one White, heterosexual female cited a "growing sense of moral and spiritual integrity." A White, heterosexual male reported that one reason he became an ally was "spiritual motivation. Faith in an inclusive deity." For none of these respondents was this their sole motivation for becoming an ally; however, spiritual beliefs and experiences were an important influence in their activities as allies.

Personal Relationships with Members of Oppressed Groups

The fifth reason identified for becoming an ally involves personal experiences with members of the nondominant group. Many allies become involved with people from diverse backgrounds and learn of the struggles they encounter. Seeing their friends oppressed often motivates allies to respond by increasing their knowledge of relevant issues and taking direct action to decrease prejudice and discrimination by others.

> I don't recall really knowing anybody that was openly gay/lesbian as I was growing up. Coming to graduate school and meeting people who were openly gay/lesbian really changed my mind about things. As I grew to care more about these individuals it was not possible in good faith to NOT become an ally. I could see first hand how dealing with homophobia really hurt the people I cared about and loved. I knew I had to do something in whatever small way, beyond just being supportive on an individual level. I also figured the world is too heterosexual, in ways that I'm just starting to understand. A few hours of going to a gay club or march is not too much of a hardship for me, given what my friends have to face on a daily basis. (African American, female, heterosexual no. 2)

> I think it was realizing that people I truly care about experience deep pain and struggle from disadvantages they suffer due to institutional, cultural, or individual forms of discrimination and oppression. (White, male, heterosexual no. 2)

Thus, Allport's (1954) Contact Theory, in which he suggests that mere contact with individuals who are markedly different from oneself is a means of breaking down stereotypes and discrimination and at least in part explains the motivation behind the actions of allies.

For most allies, however, there is not one single reason for becoming an ally. Rather, there are many reasons. Explanations often include a reference to childhood upbringing as well as personal experiences with friends and experiencing discrimination firsthand, which leads to increased sensitivity toward other groups. For some individuals, all of these explanations are offered. For example, one White, Jewish, heterosexual female described her reasons for becoming an ally as being very complex. She knew the experience of discrimination first-hand as a Jew and believed that this had led to heightened sensitivity toward other racial, religious, and persecuted groups. Her interracial marriage provided her with additional knowledge of issues related to ethnicity. Finally, she described meeting a number of gay men through her work and gaining an understanding of what she described as "antigay bigotry," which she saw attacking and impacting her close friends. Thus, she saw herself as an ally both to persons of color and to gays and lesbians.

What leads someone to become an ally? The answer appears to be multifaceted. The rich responses provided by the allies we know suggest there are many paths people may take on the road to identifying as an ally of a group. What remains unclear is whether these paths open up simultaneously or sequentially and whether the likelihood of someone's becoming an ally increases as these experiences increase. For example, many people are members of oppressed groups but do not turn around and become allies of other groups that are also oppressed. Many people have friends who belong to marginalized groups, but they do not automatically become active public advocates and allies for these groups. Is one of these experiences sufficient for some people, whereas for others it takes a combination? It also remains unclear why some individuals with certain childhood histories and personal experiences become allies in adulthood, whereas others with similar experiences do not.

In addition, why do people become allies of some groups but not of others that are equally oppressed? Why might a member of a non-dominant group describe her or his sensitivity as being based on personal experiences with discrimination and then choose to become an ally of one marginalized group but not another? It will be interesting to examine whether people become allies for certain groups in any particular order or merely as they become friends with members of various groups. For example, it is possible that a heterosexual Asian/Pacific American male may be sensitized to discrimination based on his own personal experiences and serve as an ally of women but not become an ally of gay men and lesbians until he forges personal relationships with gay men or lesbians. Although responses we gathered enlighten us about experiences allies see as having been critical to their development, important questions regarding the development of an allied identity remain.

☐ Personal Experiences of Allies

The experience of being an ally seems to differ among people. Allies we contacted provided a wide range of descriptions when asked what their own experiences as allies have been like. Most allies reported that their personal experiences have been somewhat mixed. Most allies identified positive experiences, but many also reported encountering difficulties and believed that their allied behavior had sometimes caused losses, either personally or economically.

Positive experiences resulting from being an ally may include personal enrichment, developing new friendships, and being energized and challenged.

> I have truly enjoyed this work and feel like I am at my best—like the part of me I like best comes out in this work. I have gained invaluable relationships and friendships . . . I love the challenge of working on a multicultural team. (White, female, heterosexual no. 2)

> Energizing and amazing—the opportunity to become aware of the truth in others' experiences, to participate in social justice work that may restore real relationships—is a great privilege and source of celebration, self-discovery, growth and connection across and within human differences. (White, female, lesbian no. 4)

> [My experiences have been] almost always positive. I have made many good friends in human rights and gay movements and have grown as a person through my human rights work. (Jewish American, female, heterosexual)

Serving as an ally has both inter- and intrapersonal benefits for individuals committed to these activities.

However, being an ally is not always a completely positive experience. Although no allies we know described their experiences in solely negative terms, some allies reported encountering difficulties as a result of their activist behavior. Negative experiences often included reactions from members of their own dominant group or from members of the nondominant group for whom they were trying to serve as allies.

> . . . often I am mistrusted, doubted, challenged and rejected. This has occurred in groups with target and nontarget persons. When I am

exhausted, it hurts more when targeted persons express any of the above. Nontargets, if unwilling to hear or recognize the issue I may address, are able to disqualify and attempt to discredit me. (White, female, heterosexual no. 1)

Yet for many allies, this experience is more complex, having both positive and negative consequences, and cannot be narrowly described. Although sometimes difficult and alienating, being an ally is also richly rewarding.

I've lost friends because of basic differences in beliefs; at times, I have been scared to place myself in the position of advocate—both for fear of alienation and ridicule, as well as fear of my own physical safety. On the other hand, it has also been a personally rewarding experience to know that I'm "doing my part" to break stereotypes and end oppression. (Asian/ Pacific American, male, heterosexual)

Sometimes I have been frightened of physical confrontation, [such] as when [I was] in high school, identified as a [expletive deleted], I was harassed at school [because of my African American girlfriend]. Other times, I have been exhilarated by the sense of righteousness that being on the side of justice brings. And many other times I have felt unworthy of others' trust in me as an ally, especially knowing that, as a White man, I can and have left the struggle when I so desired. (White, male, heterosexual no. 1)

Overall it has been positive. I feel blessed to be able to be a part of another group. That is, I know how hard it can be to trust someone who has heterosexual privilege. The fact that my friends would trust me enough to share their world with me, even when I don't always understand means a lot to me. . . . I've learned a lot about courage. At times it has been scary. Particularly when I feel the backlash of heterosexuals who think I might be lesbian because I'm vocal about these issues. (African American, female, heterosexual no. 2)

They've been sad, scary, enlightening, joyful, interesting, challenging, fun, hard. (White, female, bisexual)

This last statement seems an apt summary of allied experiences.

☐ How Is Allied Behavior Viewed by Members of Dominant Versus Nondominant Groups?

We suspect that serving as an ally may be regarded differently by members of one's own dominant group than it is by members of the group for whom one serves as an ally. In other words, the perception of the same allied behavior might vary according to the person observing the behavior. Allies we contacted reported that they often found this to be true.

Allies reported that they believed their allied activities were generally viewed positively and with support by members of the allied group, but that this often occurred after an initial period of mistrust and suspicion.

> Sometimes I am viewed with suspicion, particularly in a role as ally to people of color, who usually want to know whether I have made a long-term commitment to their cause or whether I am just another White person "grandstanding"—acting liberal when it's convenient, but not willing to do the hard work, make sacrifices. Once accepted, [I] have received strong support. (White, female, lesbian no. 1)

> . . . my sense is that people of color with whom I work view me as a welcome ally, but that their acceptance of me and my efforts is contingent upon me being there with them—to stand up and be counted— when real risks or sacrifices may be called for. This seems perfectly reasonable and justifiable to me. (White, male, heterosexual no. 1)

> People appreciate it, but some individuals question my motives as though affinities and alliances are only superficially driven. (Asian/Pacific American, female, heterosexual)

> Appreciated. A positive experience. (African American, female, heterosexual no.1)

> Not being trusted occurs especially early on in a relationship. More often, with time and constancy in my words and actions there is a great deal of support and appreciation received in return. Any acknowledgment is very rewarding—yet I have learned it may not be a direct response. Nor is it essential. Knowing looks, nods, smiles and friendships have been in the experiences and mean so much [they equal] reinforcement. (White, female, heterosexual no. 1)

Thus, allies often find they are viewed quite positively by members of the groups for which they serve as allies. However, this positive reaction is not automatic but results from consistent, public allied behavior. Allies often encounter suspicion and doubt initially, as might be expected. Members of the nondominant group recognize that many people can sound good on occasion or behave in a politically correct manner when it does not cost them anything or pose any possible risk. Kivel (1996) describes this wariness or initial mistrust as one of the harms resulting from racism and sexism, something that can be overcome only over time and through visible, committed allied behavior. There seems to be a sense (and an acceptance) among allies, however, that members of the allied group will view them positively and grow to trust them once they show themselves to be trustworthy.

Allies are often viewed somewhat differently, however, by members of their own dominant group. Colleagues, friends, and family members who share allied values often offer support and encouragement, and allies purposely seek out these interpersonal relationships. However, many allies we contacted reported mixed experiences with members of their own dominant group who knew of their allied activities. People who were not similarly committed to being allies often either did not understand the commitment of allies or viewed these activities negatively.

> Within [my] "true" peer group of other allies, being an ally is respected. . . . [However] other White people/peer groups usually respond with hostility, defensiveness, or fear to any real discussion of race. (White, female, lesbian no. 1)

> I think at times it is viewed negatively by Black folks. I've been told that Black people have so many problems and issues in our own community, why would I waste my time sticking up for White [gay/lesbian] people. Black people also don't seem to appreciate drawing attention to the similarities between racism and homophobia. (African American, female, heterosexual no. 2)

> Some are very supportive, others are wary and seem to see me as the "PC police," like I make them self-conscious because of what I do. Some family members are verbally supportive but seem to prefer to not talk about or know more about what I do. (White, female, heterosexual no. 2)

> For some, I think I am an inspiration. . . . For others, I am an ideologue, a boor and a bore, a "reverse" racist and, at worst, a race traitor. (White, male, heterosexual no. 1)

Thus, allies elicit quite varied reactions from those around them. There is no guarantee they will be accepted by members of the allied group, although this is often the case. In contrast, they are often questioned and challenged by members of their own group who do not understand their commitment to crossing demographic lines.

☐ What Sustains Allies in Their Efforts?

We now have a greater understanding of some of the factors that motivate people to become allies—upbringing, personal experiences of discrimination, spiritual belief, concern for justice—and know that the experience of being an ally has been both positive and negative for most allies. One question that remains is: What helps to sustain people as allies once they have committed themselves to this activity? So we asked allies this very question. Although being an ally is a deeply personal commitment, allies do share some common values that influence their experiences and thus have yielded some consistent themes in response to this question. Many of the points are similar to those that motivate some people to become allies initially, such as a sense of justice, religious or spiritual beliefs, or personal relationships. However, some allies also mentioned being sustained by the view that it is part of their identity and by the belief that the work they do is important in the world.

Personal Sense of Self

For many individuals, being an ally is simply part of who they are and they cannot imagine not engaging in allied behavior. Many allies describe it as essential to how they see themselves, as involving a personal code and set of values. The words used by the allies we contacted show how strongly they feel about their commitment and the firm sense that they could behave in no other way.

> First of all, I am built such that I cannot face life any other way. Sometimes I try not to react to bigotry, but I find I cannot be silent even though I am not happy to have my name on letters to the editor, in articles, etc. (Jewish American, female, heterosexual)

> Sometimes I don't really know. I'm not expecting any reward in the afterlife! . . . My rewards are being able to live with myself, to assuage my guilt at having much unearned privilege, and believing that I am part of the solution to what I see as being the basic problem of human greed. (White, female, lesbian no. 1)

> . . . my own personal sense that I am living in accordance with my values. (White, female, lesbian no. 2)

Related to this sense of self, yet somewhat different, was the idea that serving as an ally provided the opportunity for personal growth and fulfillment.

> . . . a continual expanding of self-awareness [through my work as an ally]. (White, male, heterosexual no. 1)

> [Serving as an ally provides] regular ways/consistent practice at restoring my self, my resolve and creating same for others in my "life." (White, female, heterosexual no. 1)

Personal Relationships

For many allies, it is the personal relationships they have made through their activities that sustains them as allies. For some allies this might involve appreciation and recognition by the targeted group; for most, however, it involves strong friendships and collegial ties.

> . . . the reward of good friendships and providing support [sustains my being an ally]. (African American, female, heterosexual no. 1)

> . . . personal relationships. . . . It is my work and friendship ties with both people across differences and within my own group, that continue to allow me to debrief negative experiences, celebrate lovely moments and challenge my "stuck" places. (White, female, lesbian no. 4)

Spiritual and Religious Beliefs

Some allies reported that their spiritual beliefs or commitment to a religious faith has helped to sustain them as allies. This may include either specific religious practices such as prayer and meditation, as cited by one White female respondent, or a more general belief that what they are doing is consistent with their spiritual beliefs. For example, one respondent stated:

> I have argued that at times being an ally is like a form of religion. You have beliefs or tenets about how to live your life and how to interact with others; you have a certain level of faith about your beliefs; and you need to continue to examine and struggle with notions of a greater good. (Asian/Pacific American, male, heterosexual)

Justice Concerns

Just as allied behavior was felt to be morally correct and motivated respondents to become allies, the focus on increasing justice in the world served as a sustaining force for their activities. A personal sense that their behavior was ethical and reflected their commitment to justice helped to sustain allies as they took on challenging activities.

> Speaking out for injustice, [and] helping people better value, understand and appreciate diversity [sustains me as an ally]. (White, female, lesbian no. 3)

> My belief that it's the right thing to do. (White, female, bisexual)

[I have a] deep-seated conviction that "this is the right thing to do"—ethics. (White, male, heterosexual no. 3)

Belief that Being an Ally Contributes to Real Change

Finally, many allies are sustained by the belief that serving as allies is some of the most important work they do and by the belief that they are helping to make real change in our world.

> [I have] a strong belief that this is good, significant, needed work. (White, female, heterosexual no. 3)

> What sustains me is . . . a sense of forging and being a part of a real human community. . . . a deep conviction that the struggle against racism and exploitation is the most important work in our time. (White, male, heterosexual no. 1)

> [I hope] to make some real changes by touching the lives of others. (African American, female, heterosexual no. 2)

In her book *The Measure of Our Success,* Marian Wright Edelman (1992) describes 25 lessons she thinks are important for our lives. Lesson 13 is "Be confident that you can make a difference" (p. 58). It is this core belief that she focuses on to keep her going when she finds herself feeling overwhelmed or when she worries, conversely, about doing enough to matter. It is a belief that seems to be important in sustaining many allies.

Thus, most allies find that many factors sustain them in their efforts. Many allies have a personal sense that their work is important and ethically just, and they describe their motivations as having an internal basis. However, they are also sustained by meaningful personal relationships and view the chance to see changes happening around them as integral to their continued perseverance as allies. This multifaceted base is probably quite useful in helping allies to maintain their activities over time. Changes or problems in any one area may be offset by experiences in another domain.

☐ What Do You Find Difficult About Being an Ally?

Although all of the allies we contacted described positive experiences as allies and continued to feel sustained in their efforts, all were able to list at least one difficulty they had encountered as allies. These difficulties generally involved three common themes: (1) not having enough time to devote to allied activities and the energy it takes to remain committed and involved; (2) feelings of frustration or hope-lessness; and (3) being viewed or treated negatively by others who do not value the allied behavior.

Time and Energy

Like most of us, allies have busy schedules, and time constraints sometimes make it hard for allies to feel satisfied with their activities.

> [One difficulty is] not being able to do everything for everyone well—not enough time to attend meetings. (White, female, lesbian no. 3)

> [My only difficulty is] finding time to be more available/supportive as an ally. (African American, female, heterosexual no. 1)

However, beyond time, it also takes energy to be an active ally, and allies sometimes become tired, especially when dealing with emotion-ally charged issues. This makes it difficult to maintain the level of activity allies often expect of themselves.

> [It is difficult] debating emotionally charged issues when I'm run down. (White, female, heterosexual no. 1)

> So many battles to fight. I am always so pleased when someone new steps forward to speak up on issues. In the antigay movement, which went on for three years very intensely [in my conservative state], I was totally exhausted, as were most of the other participants. Unfortunately, lately we have been less active than we were proactive because we burnt ourselves out with constant activities. (Jewish American, female, het-erosexual)

This ally's commitment was clear and strong, but she was obviously tired and needed more allies to lighten the load.

In addition, some respondents described the energy it takes to maintain their allied commitments when these activities are optional and not required because they already benefit from dominant group privilege.

> [I've had difficulty at times] keeping the energy and commitment going when I have the privilege/option of NOT engaging in the struggle, not reaching out to *oppressed* groups, not working to be visible as an ally on campus and in the community. (White, female, lesbian no. 4)

> [I find it a challenge] being consistent, sticking with it, not hiding be-hind my own privilege. (White, male, heterosexual no. 2)

Frustration and Feelings of Hopelessness

Some allies find that although they remain committed to being allies, they have encoutered frustration and sometimes feel hopeless about the impact of their activities on the world in which we live.

> [Sometimes, I have] a feeling of frustration when these people . . . fail to "see" or comprehend what has become patently visible to me (e.g., White racism and its privileges, etc.). (White, male, heterosexual no. 1)

> [I feel] frustration with people I care about who don't see [the] need to get involved. (White, female, heterosexual no. 1)

> Being aware of the discrimination at so many levels. There is also a sense of hopelessness at times. (African American, female, heterosexual no. 2)

Thus, although allies are often motivated by the sense that their efforts can make a real difference in society, this mood is sometimes difficult to maintain, and doubt can intrude.

Perceptions by Others and Negative Treatment

Finally, some allies experience negative interactions with other people as a result of their being allies for particular groups. At times this negative response may involve primarily undesired verbal comments or perceptions.

> [Sometimes it makes it difficult when I experience] hurtful comments and slights which often become very personal in their attack be it against an individual or group. (White, female, heterosexual no. 1)

> [It is difficult when I am] being ridiculed, threatened, or otherwise marginalized. (White, male, heterosexual no. 1)

> I know that I may be a victim of some negative experiences that my friends face (e.g., rejection, hostile comments). (African American, female, heterosexual no. 2)

However, this negative response can also include economic and physical dimensions.

> [It is difficult because of] the economic and social costs of rocking the boat. I believe being an ally has cost me in terms of salary and influence in my current job. In order to be effective, an ally has to be prepared to be unpopular and even ostracized. (White, female, lesbian no. 1)

Being seen as the PC police is tough sometimes. A sense of vulnerability when I explain what I do to someone new. Getting into arguments and/or being dismissed. (White, female, heterosexual no. 2)

On one occasion after I wrote a letter to the editor protesting a KKK rally in a conservative town where I lived, I was stalked outside of my home by a man with a baseball bat. (White, female, lesbian no. 2)

☐ Do Allies Ever Stop Being Allies, Once Involved?

An interesting area requiring further study is whether, once someone has made a commitment to being an ally and has served in this capacity she or he remains active or discontinues or changes this behavior at some future time. Allies we contacted described varied experiences. Some allies have never stopped being allies for a group, whereas others have not actually stopped being allies but have found themselves being less involved during certain periods in their lives.

[I have never completely abandoned my commitment or activities], but at times [I] have been less involved as an ally than others, depending on circumstances/specific events and my energy level. (White, female, lesbian no. 1)

I have been aware of limiting my "support," especially when I am exhausted, feeling underappreciated, unrecognized, at risk and hopeless. (White, female, heterosexual no. 1)

I don't think I've ever stopped (at least once I made the conscious decision and acknowledgment that I was an ally). However, like with anything that requires work and struggle, I have slipped and fallen back into past stereotypes and prejudices. The "unlearning" is a life-long process. (Asian/Pacific American, male, heterosexual)

Some allies, however, do stop being allies for particular groups.

Just recently [I stopped being an ally for] a student group . . . the cost was too great. (Asian/Pacific American, female, heterosexual)

[I have stopped being an ally to] all groups when I get tired. Some groups because of a struggle with my own beliefs. (White, male, heterosexual no. 2)

After my initial engagement with "the struggle" in high school . . . I felt I understood the issues, I had "done" racism. . . . For years, I paid lip service to the cause, even attending some demonstrations, but it wasn't until I saw "The Color of Fear" in 1992 that it hit me that my Whiteness, along with all the baggage that comes along with it, allowed me to walk away. Since then, I am acutely aware of numerous other little betrayals; inaction in the face of racist jokes or innuendos, etc. Realizing, though, that guilt is a paralyzing emotion, I forgive myself and vow to be more courageous and honest in the future. (White, male, heterosexual no. 1)

Thus, becoming an ally initially is no guarantee that a person will remain an ally. In addition, it appears that even those individuals with good intentions find themselves fatigued and overburdened at times, times that leave them likely to decrease their involvement in allied activities. As McIntosh (1988) indicated, that is one of the unearned privileges of not being on the downside of power.

☐ Conclusions

Being an ally is, we believe, one of the most important activities to which a person can make a commitment. Allies, through the use of privilege based on dominant group status, can speak up and work to change inequitable situations. White people talking to other White people about racism is different from African Americans or Native Americans talking to White people about these issues. Men who confront sexism against women in group settings or with other men sound different from women who do the same and are responded to differently. Heterosexuals who label homophobia and work toward equal rights for lesbians and gay men are heard in ways that are seldom possible for lesbians and gays themselves to be heard. These allies make a difference. Sometimes it is immediate; sometimes it is longer in coming. However, they reframe the status quo and encourage all of us to consider active change.

The experience of being an ally is a multifaceted, rich experience that cannot be described succinctly or easily. Although allies have much in common, no two allies are likely to be identical. Allies have various motivations for their behavior, advocate for many different groups, are sustained by numerous factors, and encounter quite different problems as a result of their commitments. Yet, allies, different as they are, share much in common. They have a concern about justice and about people and recognize their roles in working toward those goals. Allies know that their dominant or majority group status confers on them a special privilege and a special responsibility to actively support people on the downside of power and to work simultaneously to equalize unequal situations. Their commitment and efforts do matter and are important components of social change.

The development of allies is indeed an important way of overcoming resistance to multiculturalism and other areas of diversity. It is important to learn more about how those who already serve as allies can help others to develop their own identities as allies and how we can increase the number of alliances allies already hold. It is our hope that we can make progress toward creating an environment that will help to create more allies.

☐ References

Allport, G. W. (1954). *The nature of prejudice.* Reading, MA: Addison-Wesley.

Edelman, M. W. (1992). *The measure of our success: A letter to my children and yours.* New York: HarperCollins.

Kivel, P. (1996). *Uprooting racism: How White people can work for racial justice.* Philadelphia: New Society.

McIntosh, P. (1988). *White privilege and male privilege: A personal account of coming to see correspondences through work in women's studies* (Working Paper Number 189). Wellesley College, Wellesley, MA.

Tatum, B. D. (1997). *"Why are all the Black kids sitting together in the cafeteria?" and other conversations about race.* New York: Basic Books.

6
CHAPTER

Addressing Resistance in the Classroom

How often have you discussed issues of multiculturalism with people who are not ethnic minorities themselves and sensed a certain defensiveness or overaccommodation from some of those individuals? In talking with various colleagues across the country, I have found this to be a common experience. Perhaps it is because there seems to be a knee-jerk reaction based on the feeling that the discussion of such issues is a subtle accusation that these individuals are racist. This presents a challenge to those teaching cross-cultural psychology courses, as the requirement in many disciplines, such as psychology, counseling psychology, marriage and family therapy, and social work, is that all students to be exposed to cross-cultural issues in order to render them more culturally sensitive. How does one get beyond resistance from students who would otherwise never have taken a course that raised such issues? Over the years, I have tried a number of methods to get around such resistance. The following have been my attempts to address resistance; I am entirely aware that others use a wider array of interventions and discussion points. One popular alternative approach, which I do not employ, is to discuss conflict resolution models (e.g., Thomas, 1976, 1992).

☐ Racial Identity Development Models

Minority Identity Development Models

My first technique is in-depth discussions of the issues involved in racial identity. As many of you know, racial identity models have been discussed at least since the time when Cross (1971) and White (1972) presented their formal models of African Americans' moving from a "Negro" identity to a "Black" identity. As exposure to these models became more and more widespread, ethnic minorities adopted the essence of these models as the basis for all racial identity for ethnic minorities in a White majority culture (e.g., Corvin & Wiggins, 1989; Ponterotto, 1988). I present a combination of the Corvin and Wiggins (1989) and Ponterotto (1988) models to my students, which suggests that ethnic minority individuals go through four stages of identity development: pre-encounter, encounter, immersion, and internalization. Because of the familiarity with racial identity models of most readers this book, I will not go into these models in depth. However, I would like to share some of the examples I use to illustrate my points when discussing the models.

The Pre-encounter Stage

In the pre-encounter stage, ethnic minority individuals accept the dominant view that the world is nonminority or antiminority. Alternatively, they can act in ways that deny any differences between themselves (along with their ethnic minority group) and the majority group. This can be translated into a naive "people are people" attitude. Although my own view is that this is true at a deep, humanistic level, individuals in this stage accept this view naively, almost forcing similarity where similarity does not exist. In so doing, they act in ways that negate or devalue their own ethnic minority group. I try to be open about my own development. I discuss how I actually avoided studying or being an advocate for ethnic minority issues, particularly those pertaining to Japanese or Asian American concerns. I did this because I did not want to be perceived to be "riding on the coattails" of my own ethnic minority status. I also accepted the dominant view, back when I was a graduate student, that if I were to concentrate on Asian issues, my work would not be perceived to be "important" or "accepted" as mainstream research. In discussing my own resistance to multicultural issues as a graduate student, I hope to set the tone for my current students to acknowledge that they, too, may have similar resistances.

The Encounter Stage

In the encounter stage, individuals are hit with encounter that prevent them from denying any longer that they are members of an ethnic minority group, and they realize that their group *is* different from the White majority group in some important respects. The most common of these encounters deal with racism or other forms of discrimination, but there can also be positive encounters that set in motion a form of thinking that helps individuals validate themselves in terms of their ethnic minority status. A negative encounter I share was described to me by one of my former students, Dottie Morris (personal communication, March 1989). She told me of a case in New York in which an African American male tried to deny that he was any different from his White majority counterparts. He had gone to Harvard University, receiving his master's degree in business administration. Then he secured a job as a Wall Street analyst. One evening after work, he tried to hail a cab. Cab after cab kept passing him by, picking up others but not him. After about half an hour of being passed by, he finally snapped. An empty cab that had not picked him up was stopped at a traffic light. This MBA Wall Street analyst leaped onto the hood of the cab and started beating it with his briefcase. Of course, he was arrested and sentenced to do community service and seek counseling. In this encounter, he realized that there was something about his ethnicity that made him different from all those individuals who were successful in hailing cabs.

My own encounter occurred when I was a professor (I try to invite students to discuss their naiveté about these issues by admitting that my own awareness came relatively late in my development as a mental health professional). Although I had been exposed to issues of multiculturalism, I had not been moved by them. While a professor at Washington State University, I attended a men's conference held on campus. I was quite impressed with one of the speakers, Harry Brod. Near the end of his presentation, he discussed the importance of male identity, which went hand in hand with ethnic minority identity. As he elaborated on this point, I began to realize how much I had missed by not fully pursuing issues involving my own Japanese American/ Asian/Pacific American identity. At that point, I was developing the cross-cultural psychology course to be taught in my department, and I began to understand at a deeper level the importance of these issues. This clearly helped me to develop a much better course than I would otherwise have developed.

Another positive encounter I relate to my students is my self-observation when Nelson Mandela was released from prison. I remember seeing him walking down the road waving to the crowd, and I thought, "Oh, how sad. Look how old he is. His government robbed him of so many years!" Later, when I saw the many interviews he conducted after his release, I began to have a very different opinion. I remember thinking how dignified he was in the way he presented himself, and I can honestly say that it was one of those moments when I was glad to be alive to witness such an occasion. I truly felt uplifted by his dignity and spirit. Because of my sensitivity to these issues, I also remember thinking that if I were Black, it would be one of those positive encounter moments that would help me to validate myself in terms of my African American identity.

The Immersion Stage

In the immersion stage, individuals reject all values not synchronous with their own ethnic minority values. They try to immerse themselves fully in their own minority culture. In this stage, their identities are dependent upon others' identities, as they quite often compare their own development with that of others in their ethnic minority group. Back in the 1960s and 1970s, I recall the expression "blacker than thou," which was used to describe the way some African Americans tried to prove their allegiance to their ethnic minority culture by trying to be more black than others in their group. I remember that when *Shogun* was a bestseller (Clavell, 1979), many Japanese Americans I knew tried to compare one another's understanding of the deeper meanings of passages in the novel. This, too, was a way of being "more Japanese than thou." However, ultimately, this stage is not fully satisfying for at least two reasons. First, because we live in a White majority society, it is not in our own best interest to reject the majority of the population, given that all of the established institutions are grounded in that society. Second, our identities are not based on a secure sense of self but rather on comparison with others in our group, and there exists the need to denigrate others so we can have a sense of our own identities. Typically, I receive understanding nods from my students about the unsatisfying nature of this stage.

The Internalization Stage

The internalization stage occurs when individuals develop a secure sense of self as an ethnic minority member. An implication of this is that they can express preferences for and interests in experiences of the White majority population and other ethnic minority populations without fear that it will impact negatively on their sense of their own ethnicity. Again, I do a little self-disclosure by telling students that I was the chair of the board of directors of the local ballet and performing arts committee. This expression of support for a Eurocentric dance form did not threaten my sense of being someone of Japanese/Asian descent.

Majority Identity Development Models

The majority identity development models that have been created (e.g., Corvin & Wiggins, 1989; Helms, 1990; Ponterotto, 1988) parallel the minority identity development models. Again, I use a combination of the Corvin and Wiggins (1989) and Ponterotto (1988) models, principally because these models are directly comparable to the original Cross (1971) and White (1972) models of Black identity development. There are also four stages in these models—pre-exposure, exposure, zealot-defensive, and integration—and again, I present them here only as a backdrop for the stories I tell my students to help them understand the applicability of these stages to their own development.

The Pre-exposure Stage

The pre-exposure stage here is comparable to the pre-encounter stage of the minority identity development models. There is a naive people-are-people attitude, and little thought has been given to issues of multiculturalism. In thinking that people are people, individuals at this stage are really thinking "people are like me and those familiar to me." There is a denial that racism exists in society, or at least a minimization of racism's existence. Moreover, these individuals have not even considered their own majority group status and what that entails.

The Exposure Stage

In the exposure stage, individuals are confronted with the realities of racism and discrimination. They learn how the European-American view has been taken for granted as the "only" or the "proper" view, and they must confront the ways in which their own naive acceptance of this view has helped to perpetuate racism in society. They typically have two reactions: anger and guilt. They feel angry about having been duped into accepting the notion that past ways of conceptualizing the world have been fair and just. They feel guilty because they realize how their naive acceptance of the fairness view has been fostering subtle racism. At this point, I ask students what the Great Compromise of the 1787 Constitutional Congress was. Most students do not know, but they are familiar with it when I discuss it. This compromise was the division of Congress into two houses, one based upon equal representation (the Senate) and the other based upon the size of each state (the House of Representatives). This initial compromise did not satisfy the Southern, slave-owning states. They argued that although slaves were not "real people," they still increased the population size of the Southern states. Therefore, it was written into the Constitution that slaves would count as three fifths of a human being in order to increase the representation these Southern states would have in the U.S. Congress. This reminder opens up the eyes of many of my students, as it offers proof that from the very beginning, non-Whites were not considered human beings, or at least not human beings on a par with White majority individuals. This three fifths concept resurfaced in western states, where they wanted to count Asian immigrants as three fifths of a human being so they could increase the West's representation in Congress.

The Zealot-Defensive Stage

The next stage, the zealot-defensive stage, causes one of two reactions in White majority individuals. Either they become zealots for ethnic minority causes or they become defensive about the majority culture view or even withdraw altogether from finding out about other cultures. In becoming zealots, individuals seem to be reacting to their own guilt about their naive acceptance of the way things are. They become other-focused in that they compare what they are doing to support ethnic minority causes with what others are doing. If they are doing more, they feel better about themselves by making the comparison and even put others down for not understanding or doing more about the issues. In becoming defensive, individuals attempt to have contact only with their own majority culture or they try to defend themselves and the majority culture by pointing to all of the "concessions" made by the majority culture to the minority cultures. Obviously, as this society becomes more and more multicultural, it becomes more and more difficult to have contact only with one's own culture. Pointing out the so-called concessions made by the majority culture makes it difficult to deny that there was some disparity in the way others were treated. This becomes an admission of the unfairness in society.

The Integration Stage

Finally, the integration stage is comparable to the internalization stage of the minority identity development models. The overly strong feelings of the previous stage have subsided, and a more balanced view takes their place. Ironically, a deeper appreciation of one's own culture occurs with the acceptance, both intellectually and emotionally, of other cultures. From this deeper appreciation of one's own culture, one can be secure and self-confident, which allows for an acceptance of all cultures. I also discuss how people typically cycle through these stages (Parham, 1989); at times they feel they have reached the final stage, but then some new exposure cycles them back through the exposure, zealot-defensive, and integration stages.

After a discussion of minority and majority identity development models, I tell a story about a friend of mine, Kathleen, whose son was asking strange questions. He was in the first grade, and he came home one day and asked, "Mommy, are we Black?" Kathleen said, "No, Mr. Smith is Black, and Ms. King is Black, but we're not Black." The next day, Kathleen's son asked, "Mommy, are we Jewish?" Kathleen said, "No, Ms. Cohen is Jewish, and Mr. Rosenberg is Jewish, but we're not Jewish." Kathleen was wondering why her son was coming home with these strange questions, so she went to school with him the next day and asked his teacher why he was asking such questions. His teacher explained that it was cultural awareness week in her class. Immediately, Kathleen knew that her son was asking, "Mommy, what are we?" That night, she was prepared. When her son came home, she said, "Tommy, we are Irish!" She cooked a corned beef and cabbage dinner, and they read various Irish tales. He was quite pleased that he finally knew what he was.

I further try to make the issue even more relevant to individuals belonging to the majority culture by connecting culture tales to the transmission of cultural values. I then present a culture tale that is particularly resonant for me. The essence of the story is the close relationship between a boy and his grandfather. However, the grandfather gets old and becomes frail. This causes him to drop one of the fine porcelain rice bowls during dinner on a number of occasions. With each successive broken rice bowl, the boy's father becomes more and more upset until finally, he banishes the grandfather from the dinner table, saying that he can eat only table scraps after the rest of the family has eaten. The next day, the father finds his son crying and carving something out of wood. When the father asks his son what he is doing, the son says, "I am carving a rice bowl made of wood because when I grow up, I want you to be able to eat dinner with my family."

After presenting this story, I discuss how all cultures have culture tales, each being as important to its respective culture as all other cultures' tales are to theirs. In so doing, I hope to transmit respect for other cultures as well as to convey the importance of discovering one's own roots, thereby feeling more comfortable with oneself, which allows one to feel more comfortable with others. Recently, I asked students to write down culture tales, sayings, or proverbs that were particularly resonant for them. A few of these stories follow. (I have corrected the spelling, but the grammar, word usage, and so forth have been left intact.)

> "Value your accomplishments." This was passed down from my mother's side of the family. No matter what it may be, take pride in what you do. This is how I read into what she has always said. My family didn't have a lot to grow up with, and not much has changed, but what we had, we cherished. I believe that it is because of those words that I am finishing college. I will be the first member of my entire family, including aunts, uncles, cousins & anyone else who claims us as family to graduate from a university. Because of those words, I feel they have always given me a push to strive for this completion. Those three words have always been in the back of my mind. (White male no. 1)

> I cannot think of any particular story but I know that my mother and both my grandmothers are constantly transmitting religious stories. My family and I believe families of Mexican descent are centered on strong religious beliefs. The stories they tell reflect a strong Catholic following. The stories are mostly centered on how a particular saint came to be a saint or how someone was facing a dangerous situation and whole-heartedly asked a particular saint for help and the saint intervened and saved the person's life. I have a really close attachment to my mother and we sit for hours talking about different things and it is a great feeling to hear my mother transmit her cultural background and childhood upbringing, especially since I did not grow up with my grandparents or in Mexico where I was born. . . . I feel like I learn more from listening to their stories than I can ever learn from book or school. But it feels like a different kind of learning. I feel like I am learning about my roots and it helps me to identify with my heritage. It's as if they are telling me about myself; a side of me that I did not conceive of but that I have fully integrated. I feel like a bond has been made and I feel like a better and more knowledgeable person because of it. (Latina female no. 1)

> My mom also used to tell me that each person is provided with one bag of tears. Once we are finished with the bag of tears, we won't get any-more. She said that people should not waste their tears on something not worth crying about. People should save it for special times such as a happy occasion. This actually worked on me when I was young. I actu-ally did not cry as much because I did not want to waste my tears. (Asian/Pacific female no. 2)

> When I was attending elementary school in Hong Kong, I remember my Chinese language teacher always like to tell us old Chinese story. The story that I remember the most was about how a young and poor kid became a great scholar. The kid's family is basically really poor. And the father couldn't afford to send him to any formal school. But the child is very studious and really want to learn how to read and write. During the

daytime, he would have to help his father working on the rice field. And the only free time that he has is after dark. This is the only time that he can study. But his family is so poor that they couldn't even afford to have an oil lamp. He has to make the effort and go out to the field and catch fireflies. He would have to spend hours in catching the fireflies and put them in a little bag to use as a lamp. During the wintertime, he would have to go outside and stand under the lantern in front of those wealthy landlord's house. He would do this even in the coldest winter night. He endured all this hardship for years and finally he has passed the imperial examination. Then he became a great scholar and a high-ranking official. (Asian/Pacific male no. 1)

There was a story that my father used to say and I must have listened to this story hundreds of time. The story was about a young boxer that learn everything from his master and finally claimed that he was better than him. Most of his friends believe him but his father insist on that the master knows the boxing better than you. In order to find out, they held a matching game. He had so much confidence in himself that he did not think it twice. In the matching he lost to the master and because the master illustrated untold and unshowed tricks and moves. Although the impact of the story on me was great at the first time, he told it to me in any occasion that I displayed stubbornness and nonlistening behavior. Before the story I was a very active, talkative kid and I thought that I'm always right on any issue that was being discussed. After listening to my father story I still thought that I'm right, however, I tend to pay more attention to other people, especially elders. I still have the same feeling as I heard the story for the first time that was maybe my father knows something that I don't know or he is hiding something and waiting to turn over the winning card. (Middle Eastern male no. 1)

There was a little boy who only lived with his mom (or maybe his dad too but that was never mentioned). Since he was his mother's one and only son and child, she spoiled him to death. She let him get away with everything. He would beat up other kids, steal other kids' toys, steal items from stores, and school, kill insects and bugs. The point is, he got away with everything. Anytime he would come home to tell his mom what had happened, she would appraise him and say, "Oh that's OK son, you are still the best." The boy grew older. He became a criminal. He was robbing banks and stores. One day, he was finally caught by the police and his sentence was death by hanging (this was in Burma so the punishment does fit the crime there). As he stood upon the scaffold, the policeman asked him if he had any last words. His mother was bawling on the ground, not knowing what happened. The boy said, "Yes, I have one last thing to say to my mother." He wanted to tell her privately in her ear. The mother put her ear close to his mouth to listen to his last whisper. The boy softly says, "This is for not teaching me right from wrong" and then he violently bit off her ear and he was instantly hanged.

> Maybe this tale was kinda violent to hear as a child, but it did teach me a lesson. . . . I used to live in fear that I was going to bite her ears off, but I know now that I am above that. This story emphasized the Asian value that parents are supposed to teach their children morals. (Asian/Pacific female no. 3)

Biracial Identity Development Models

Finally, I present a biracial identity development model presented by Poston (1990). This model is similar to the minority and majority identity development models, but it has an extra stage in it in which individuals gravitate toward one racial group or another. The stages of this model are personal identity, choice of group categorization, enmeshment/denial, appreciation, and integration.

The Personal Identity Stage

In the personal identity stage, individuals develop their identities independent of their racial or ethnic backgrounds. At this point, their reference group orientations (RGOs) have not yet developed.

The Choice of Group Categorization Stage

The next stage, the choice of group categorization stage, is the stage that is most different from those previously discussed. Here, biracial children are pushed to choose one of the groups of their ethnicity over the other. Hall (1980) identified three sources of influence on choice of RGO: (1) status, (2) social support, and (3) personal reasons. Quite often, if one ethnic minority group has a higher status in the culture at large, individuals gravitate toward that culture. Thus, their RGO is toward that group. In this society, European Americans have more status and power, and many biracial individuals choose to identify with a White identity and select predominantly White friends. However, sometimes those in a particular group tend to reject others who are of mixed ethnic heritage, whereas those in another group give an individual social support for the struggles through which the individual is going. A colleague told me of a freshman at her university where she was an undergraduate peer counselor who was having some real difficulties adjusting to the identity that was being thrust upon him. He was a product of an African American and European American marriage. Throughout his entire life, he was brought up as being White, and his own personal identity was that of a White male. However, when he went to college, the White students rejected him, and the African American students acted as though he was African American himself. In other words, his chosen RGO was White, but society was thrusting upon him an African American RGO, and it was the African American students who were giving him social support at the school. Thus, "choice" of group categorization may be a misnomer in that sometimes individuals do not have an opportunity to make their own choices. Finally, by a personal source of group categorization, it is meant that other factors such as resonance with the philosophy of one group over that of the other may play a major role in the RGO selected.

The Enmeshment/Denial Stage

In the enmeshment/denial stage, there is confusion and guilt about having to choose one ethnicity over the other, because this choice carries with it some inherent rejection of one parent. Poston contends that individuals in this stage are often characterized by self-hate because of this rejection. When presenting identity development models at a colloquium, I remember a student's retelling a dramatic story about one of her friends of mixed ethnic heritage who had rejected her European American roots. She said that in another venue, the facilitator had insisted that this woman own the part of her that she was rejecting, but the woman had so rejected her European American roots that she could not conceivably accept that part, and she cried and cried because of the facilitator's insistence. For weeks after this encounter, this woman expressed the pain she was feeling about conceiving of herself as being part White.

The Appreciation Stage

In the appreciation stage, individuals begin to appreciate their multiple identities and to broaden their RGOs to include other ethnic groups previously rejected. The feelings of self-hate begin to be resolved, and in this stage, individuals begin to appreciate what these other groups have to offer.

The Integration Stage

Finally, the integration stage sees individuals more fully appreciating their multicultural identities and existence. This integration allows them to have secure identities. On that basis, they can interact with others.

☐ Reaction Papers

A second technique I use to make people feel at ease about discussing cross-cultural issues is to assign a required, weekly "reaction paper." The instructions for this paper give students a wide berth. They can write about anything dealing with cross-cultural issues, such as a class discussion, one of the readings for the week, a current event, or something that stimulates a childhood memory. They can write about anything, and my only requirement is that they write about something involving cross-cultural issues, be it positive or negative. Their grades have nothing to do with the actual content of their papers, only that they complete them each week. I give students one break week, should they choose to use it. This break week can be used at times when the students are on vacation, when they have other pressing course problems, when they have family matters to attend to, or when they have simply forgotten to do the assignment; thereafter, I assess a heavy penalty for each successive paper missed. I tell them that I will keep their reaction papers confidential. I do this because I realize that many people hold fairly culturally insensitive feelings, and I anticipate that many would not express these ideas in class discussion. These reaction papers give students an opportunity to express their ideas in a safe context. It also gives me a chance to respond to these ideas and to try to reason with the students or to present evidence counter to their positions.

Lest you feel that students still would not express culturally insensitive or racist opinions, even in this context, let me present reactions from three former students (these comments are paraphrased from the students, as I am no longer in contact with them).

> Sue and Sue are quite emotional in their writings. This indicates to me that they are overly invested in their work. Because of this, it is obvious that they are not very scientific in their writing, and their work lacks credibility. . . .
>
> Their citation practices are completely unprofessional. Instead of expressing their opinions, they cite their past work as truth to make the point they wanted to express as opinion. Moreover, they cite far too many of their past articles. No self-respecting professionals would ever cite so much of their own work. I think that they have a grandiose opinion of their own work.
>
> Finally, the Sues are too blunt and undiplomatic. Our society is no more racist than any other society in the world, but even if it were, the way in which the Sues point it out will undoubtedly further entrench the establishment's defensiveness. Thus, the Sues' blatant hostility will be taken as inflammatory and ultimately be unsuccessful. They don't

come across as reasonable or level-headed, and no one will ever listen to the suggestions they propose. (White male no. 5, criticizing the Sue and Sue (1990) textbook we were using for the course)

As I indicated, this format allows me a chance to respond to the students' comments. With respect to this student, I pointed out that many people in a wide range of areas seem to cite themselves heavily, and it was curious that he had such a strong reaction to this material. Could it be that his reaction was to the content of the material as opposed to the way in which it was presented? I also pointed out that the Sue brothers were among the pioneers in this field, and they are heavily cited by many cross-cultural writers. For them to have not cited some of their past work would have been a disservice to their book and to the students. In addition, this student was perhaps unaware that many of the references to Sue articles were to those of Stanley Sue, a Sue brother who was not one of the coauthors of the text.

This student was the most openly hostile, defensive student I have had, although he covered it up in class discussions. This next student was much more subtly resistant and perhaps reflects a point of view that occurs more frequently:

"The coloreds have taken over all of basketball!" My grandfather made this statement while watching a basketball game on television. His use of "colored" for "black" is pejorative, although probably harmless. However, I am walking on eggshells because I don't know if when I use the term "black" instead of "African American" I am offending someone. I am particularly worried that someone might hear me saying "Oriental" instead of "Asian American."

How do we decide what to call ethnic groups? I am called a "white," yet my skin color looks as white as an African American's skin looks black. Should I call myself Euro-American? That doesn't sound very good to me, nor do I even accept it as a label. I guess groups decide for themselves what to call themselves. Where are these groups, and how is it that they are deciding? Do they take a formal vote? Why do African Americans, who have only remote ancestral ties to Africa 10 or 15 generations ago, feel they must call themselves "African Americans"? (White male no. 6)

This student was much more of a challenge, for throughout the term, he would say things that were politically correct but emotionally vacuous. He seemed to be what Lillian Comas-Díaz (e.g., Comas-Díaz & Jacobson, 1991) would call a "cultural anthropologist." He resisted being affected by the material although, to his credit, he did show signs of self-examination when we discussed the racial identity material.

It is not only males who are resistant to multicultural issues. The following is an excerpt from a White female student who was highly critical of my undergraduate course in cross-cultural psychology:

> Once again, I am feeling like because I am white, I am automatically priviledged, prejudiced, you name it. I am truly sick of it. . . . Enough of the "Oh poor me. I'm a minority. I want to step on all the white people & make them pay for my hardships." Saying that one will look at all of the qualifications, and then if they are equal, look at the background (which means race) to decide, is ridiculous and unfair. It is discrimina-tion against *any* other race that did not get in because they weren't "that" race. (White female no. 2, after a class discussion on affirmative action policies)

So how can I assess the effectiveness of this technique? The vast majority of students who take my courses in cross-cultural psychology like this assignment—especially as it is presented as an alternative to writing a term paper. We are able to interact on a more personal basis through these papers. Some students who were quite hesitant to open up in the context of the class openly enjoyed the weekly "discussions" we would hold via the reaction papers. As I said, White male no. 6 was subtly resistant, and I am not sure how I changed him throughout the term, but he did demonstrate some receptivity to the racial iden-tity topic. By term's end, White male no. 5, the openly hostile student, seemed to change a bit, as measured by his final reaction paper:

> I must admit, this was my most trying course because I had not yet been exposed to most of the material. As you can tell from my reaction papers throughout the semester, I don't agree with the way some multicultural *committed* advocates present their views. White students like myself may never have had to examine their own racial identities, etc., and to have to confront this for the first time in the face of relentless pressure is challenging and painful. Why do I have to adopt such negative stereo-types of whites who have past sins?
> Ultimately, I am glad I took this course. I can really see how it will help me in the future in this profession. I will be much less biased in the future because I gained a great deal of cultural sensitivity in this course. After all, aren't we all minorities to some extent? (White male no. 5)

Although I had detected a shift in this student's attitude near the end of the term, I would have not known the extent to which he was affected had I not used this technique to teach, interact, and measure students.

I would like to finish this section by presenting a White female's final reaction paper that I received one term. I do not believe I could more eloquently present my purpose in having students perform this weekly task. This student had been quite transparently hostile toward multicultural issues throughout most of the term and was even more hostile about the reaction paper assignment. However, in her final reaction paper, she wrote:

> I have to admit I really did not look forward to these reaction papers. They were never difficult assignments, but more like weekly thorns in my side. It was hard to decide on what to write given the open-endedness of the assignments. The topics to cover were generally ones that upset me in one way or another. My reactions were generally that of disagreement with the "problem" or the realization that the problem was so pervasive that I know I can do nothing about it alone. I made a negative association with doing these assignments.
>
> Another thing that bothered me was that I did not see the point of it. What am I getting out of writing about topics related to unjustness in the world, once a week, and for 1–2 pages? Then over the past several weeks, I have noticed that there are so many things to write about, that I never was at a loss for a topic. In fact, the problem became one of "which one do I discuss?" And in the past two weeks or so, it hit me. I think that at least one of the points you had in mind for us in assigning these papers was to heighten our sensitivity and awareness. I am embarrassed and astounded at how often and how many instances of possible topics come up in my everyday life. When I listen to the radio, watch TV, in my interactions at work, or even just running around doing errands, I am almost constantly noticing things that I never paid attention to before. I have also become more aware of my style of relating and speaking, and that I have my own prejudices that at first I did not notice. Then I thought of them as subtle. Now I am working on correcting them. It is interesting how something I thought of as a "thorn in my side" has really taught me something about my world and myself. So I guess I owe you both an apology and a "thank you." (White female no. 6)

☐ Game Show or Debate Contest

When I began to implement the weekly reaction paper assignment, I had another purpose in mind. I began to think that it might be a way of measuring the effectiveness of the semester-long experience the students were to have.

At the beginning of the semester, students are divided into ethnic minority groups; they choose a group or a group is assigned to them. The only limitation is that they are not to choose their own group if they themselves are of an ethnic minority. The groups are the standard ones most cross-cultural texts use—Latino, African American, Native American, and Asian. I inform the students that they are going to engage in a debate or a game show at the end of the semester. The game matches one group against another group for the first half of week 14, then the other groups against each other for the second half of week 14. The "losers" face one another during the first half of week 15, and then the "winners" meet for the second half of week 15. This results in a ranking of the groups from first through fourth with respect to their abilities to answer questions about their respective groups. These questions were to be general questions like "How does your group understand the notion of time?" or group-specific questions like "What is the notion of 'reciprocal obligation?'" for the students assigned to the African American group. I give students samples of the general and specific questions in order to give them an opportunity to study the information that might be asked of them. I also encourage them to make up questions I might ask. I suggest that they get together outside of class to share ideas, reading materials, experiences, and anything else that might help them to perform well on this task.

The semester itself is divided into three unequal sections. The first 7 weeks of the semester are spent on general multicultural issues. Most of the assigned readings are given during this period, and the first part of the text, which deals with general issues, is also assigned. The next 6 weeks concentrate on the four specific ethnic minority groups. This section is more experiential in nature, as I select videotapes about the specific groups and also have representatives of specific ethnic minorities make presentations to the class. For example, one semester, the Native American student counselor agreed to make a presentation to my class to discuss her background and what various symbols mean to her, such as her tribe's symbol of a turtle. The class watched a videotape of "The Spirit of Crazy Horse," which depicts the standoff at the Pine Ridge Indian Reservation between the Ogalala Sioux and FBI agents and describes how it came about and how it can be understood within the context of the abuse Native Americans have encountered over the years. I also assign the reading of a few "seed" articles and chapters to get students started on finding material about their assigned groups. I remind students that they should be meeting in earnest at this point, as the debates are about to begin.

The last 2 weeks of the semester are reserved for the debates. In the few weeks leading up to this section, I remind students that they should be meeting to discuss the material they have found on their assigned ethnic minority group. I also remind them that this assignment should be considered to be in place of a term paper, so their efforts should be commensurate with that applied to a paper. Groups facing one another are determined by rolling dice. The highest number is matched with the lowest number. These groups face one another during the first half of week 14, and the other two groups face one another during the second half of week 14. After each contest, members of the nonparticipating groups vote on which of the two participating groups seems to command a better grasp of the material specific to their respective groups. This is done with the participating groups out of the room. As stated above, winners face one another in week 15, as do the losers.

After the final debate, I have students discuss how they felt during the debate process. I then ask students to contemplate four questions: (1) Did you feel empathy for your group of study? (2) Did you feel closer to other students in the group? (3) How did you feel when you had to vote for or against other students? (4) What if the consequences had been much more meaningful—that is, not simply winning a contest in a class but getting a grade in the class, entering college, or securing a highly desirable job? I discuss how these issues are connected to the contact hypothesis (e.g., Allport, 1954; Cook, 1984, 1985; Pettigrew, 1981) and to individualism and collectivism (e.g., Triandis, 1989, 1995).

My assumption, which has been confirmed by students over the years, has been that a student will feel more empathy for the group being studied because he or she knows more about that group. For example, during the debriefing in one class, a student who had studied African Americans said, "It is clear that African Americans have suffered much more than any other group we've studied." A student from the Native American group strenuously dissented. Students did tend to feel closer to the other students within their group, although this was not a strong sentiment, as students felt closer to all the other students in the class. This was reflected in some students' responses to my third question about voting for or against their colleagues in the other groups to determine winners and losers. For example, when I first discussed this debate/game show idea with students one year, a student who was a former football player and particularly competitive said, "Great! I'd love to crush my opponents." When it actually came down to voting, he protested strenuously, saying that he did not like the feeling of having to judge his classmates. (I made a mental note, wondering if he felt more empathy for me because I have to give grades to students.) Finally, students seem to agree that if the consequences were much more meaningful, they might find ways to cheat or otherwise bend the rules to their advantage.

I remind students of an issue we had discussed earlier in the quarter: if one is an inner-city African American male between the ages of 15 and 25, one has a 1 in 15 chance of being murdered. What kind of pressure are we, as a society, placing on these boys when we give them the message that the only way they can escape their situation is by playing college basketball and making it to the NBA? Fortunately, many people are now recognizing how unrealistic this goal is and how much pressure we are placing on these youngsters, and we are beginning to discuss alternative ways of allowing them to improve their lives. However, the basketball route is still a powerful one that encourages many inner-city youths to expend a great deal of time and energy on practicing and playing basketball and to bend the rules when trying to get college scholarships and asking teachers and administrators to assist in the process.

Originally, I had intended the reaction papers to be a way of measuring how students experienced the debates. By far, the best year for measuring this was the first year I implemented the debate format. At that point, many of the other departments were not yet teaching cross-cultural courses or they were just being developed, so students in other departments were inclined to take my course, which meant I had students from my own psychology department as well as from the School of Communications and the School of Education. Also, by some quirk of scheduling, more students in my own department took this particular course that year than any other year. Overall, I had 14 students in the course that year, yielding three or four students for each of the four ethnic minority groups to be assigned. I was going to take the last reaction paper of the term, to be written after the final debate and the class discussion of the process, as a measure of the effectiveness of this technique. Unfortunately, the week of our final class meeting, the first Rodney King decision and the subsequent riots in Los Angeles dominated the news. Nearly all of the students wrote about the riots as the topic of their last reaction paper.

The two subsequent years saw enrollments of 6 and 10 students in my cross-cultural classes, so there were groups of one or two in the first year and of two or three in the second. Certainly, a "group" of one is not conducive to studying group cohesiveness, and a group of two is also suspect in this area. I then left Washington State University, and I have not been able to transfer the debate format to my new institution, which operates on a 10-week quarter system. I still believe this format is an excellent one for teaching courses of this nature. I have excerpted responses of students who had written their reaction papers before the Rodney King riots in that first year and of students who were part of two- and three-member groups in the next two years. The exact wording in their reaction papers has been changed because I am no longer in contact with these students and do not have their permission to quote them directly.

> The "debates" were interesting and enjoyable. The format is perfect for a course such as this. I think that we (the students) learned as much from studying for the debates as we would have from studying for a final examination. (White female no. 7)

> In preparing for the debates, I learned much more about the history and oppression of Blacks than I ever had known before. The debates also demonstrated the issues of individualism and collectivism quite well. Working with a "team" in preparing for the debates demonstrated for me how difficult it must be for people who come from a collectivistic background to work with individualists here in America. (White male no. 7)

> The single word that would describe our first class session of debates would be "unnerving." (White female no. 8)

> I really enjoyed the class. It was a lot of fun working with my group because it helped me get to know some of my classmates better. I was impressed with how well we worked together, and we made an excellent team. (White female no. 9)

> Wow! Can I relax, now that the debates are over! Everyone in my group worked really well together, and I think that we did a terrific job of getting to know both the material and ourselves. I thought that this was a great class. (White female no. 10)

> I hated voting on my classmates' and friends' performance! A few of us even got together and talked about absolutely refusing to vote the second week. However, we worried that this might upset you, so we decided to follow your request. It was reassuring to find out that voting was part of your plan, that you used it as a device to illustrate group division. We all got the message. (White female no. 11)

As you can see, these comments are right in line with my hopes for this exercise. However, because of the limited number of such reactions, I cannot go beyond saying that these comments are only supportive of my intentions. I would be very interested to know about it if others implement these procedures and find similar results. I offer this exercise for your use and welcome your feedback.

☐ Personal Experience

At least since the time of Allport (1954), people have been discussing personal contact among differing ethnic minority groups as a method of breaking down racial barriers. One of my first attempts to get students to break down racial barriers involved a fortuitously timed program promoted by California State University, Fullerton, back in the spring of 1986. At that time, there were a number of Vietnamese refugee and first-generation Mexican American students on campus. Noticing the recent influx, the university decided to begin a Partners Program, in which they would pair up an ethnic minority student with a student not from an ethnic minority group (or, in the case of a many-generation Mexican American college student, with one of the Vietnamese students). I had given my students the option of being paired up in the Partners Program or conducting library research on an ethnic minority group and then engaging in at least five participant observations of that group. Students in the Partners Program similarly met at least five times with their partners. All students were to write a term paper on their respective experiences. As I reported (Mio, 1989), students who participated in the Partners Program seemed to have gained a much deeper understanding of the ethnic minority group in question. "This form of cross-cultural contact seems to be even more effective than a breadth of experiences with a culture if the breadth remains at a casual level. It is the depth of experience that seems to be the key factor to the enrichment of cross-cultural sensitivity" (Mio, 1989, p. 43).

☐ Resistance Among Ethnic Minority Students

In my experience, some ethnic minority students have also demonstrated resistance to examining multicultural issues. The resistance can be divided into three categories: pre-encounter-stage resistance, as contemplated by the racial identity development models, being-an-educator resistance, and simple getting-out-of-work resistance.

Pre-encounter-stage Resistance

In many respects, pre-encounter-stage resistance is the easiest to address, for it is the same kind of resistance experienced by White majority students. Many ethnic minority students who have never considered their ethnicities to be at the root of various difficulties they have encountered may deny that racial/ethnic issues are a problem for them. Thus, it is my job to ready them for an encounter experience, which sometimes occurs as a result of the course and sometimes occurs after the class has ended. As I mentioned in Chapter 3, an Asian/Pacific male who had never considered himself to be disadvantaged because of his minority status was firmly against affirmative action. He learned during the course of our classroom discussions that his thoughts about the issue were based entirely on conservative arguments that had little or no data to back up their positions. When he turned in his term paper, he had a broad smile on his face and he informed me that he had completely changed his initial position on affirmative action. He made this pronouncement with pride, as if he had had an enlightening experience.

Moments like that certainly make my work in the multicultural domain worthwhile, but I do not always come away with such success stories. Many ethnic minorities do not experience recognizable (at least to them) racism, subtle or otherwise. They prefer to keep their lives uncomplicated and are even upset with those of us teaching multicultural courses for stirring up difficult, complicating issues. I personally have never encountered extreme reactions of this nature. However, I am a member of a listserv for the Asian American Psychological Association. One of the members asked for help in dealing with this issue. She was encountering a full frontal assault by two ethnic minority students who sat in the back of the room with scowls on their faces, not say anything publicly unless it was a critical comment about racism or other multicultural issues. They would go to the professor's office to express their dissatisfaction about her bringing these issues to the surface. Her plea for help led to a flurry of responses, either affirming that these issues were arising in their own courses or suggesting ways of overcoming the resistances.

Although the Comas-Díaz and Jacobsen (1991) article concerned client–therapist forms of interaction, their conceptualization seems applicable to the student–instructor relationship, too. They might say that the reaction of these students is a cultural transference form of resistance. Issues such as seeing the instructor as a traitor for buying into the majority system of oppression, or feelings of autoracism or ambivalence are stirred in the individual. Consequently, the student may resent the instructor for being the stimulus for these feelings. Similarly, the instructor may experience a paralyzing countertransference reaction. Issues such as ambivalence, anger, or survivor's guilt may arise. Being aware of one's own countertransference reaction, the instructor may be overly sensitive to anything that might be perceived as an overreaction. Consequently, inaction may result. My only suggestion for overcoming such inaction is to consult with colleagues to ease one's mind about any course of action in which the instructor may embark.

Being-an-Educator Resistance

As most people will agree, one of the best ways of understanding multicultural issues is to openly discuss one's own thoughts, feelings, and understandings. In this way, it is possible to compare one's ideas, debate them, defend them, and perhaps modify them. Often, ethnic minorities fail to participate in such discussions because they are tired of being "educators" for the rest of the class (Jackson, 1996). This is particularly true when the number of students of color is low, not only in the particular course but in the university in general. These students feel they are always put in the position of educating the White majority students, and they are resentful that the students have not put in the time to examine such issues on their own. A corollary to this is that because they are such a small minority in these settings, there is additional pressure of being assumed to be speaking for their entire ethnic minority group, which assumption is implicit in other students' questions.

I do not have a suggestion about how to overcome such reactions; the instructor must simply be aware of such reaction, both in ethnic minority students and in their classmates. One way of showing sensitivity to this situation is to constantly and publicly remind students that an individual can speak only for himself or herself, not for an entire group. It might also be helpful to speak with the student individually in your office and remind the student that a part of the grade for the course (at least, in the case of my courses) is determined by class participation. You might also note that the student may be missing out on a valuable learning experience by not participating.

Getting-Out-of-Work Resistance

Whenever ethnic minority students try to get out of taking my multicultural courses, it is perhaps the most difficult issue for me to address because of my own personal disappointment in the students. Of course, this is my own countertransference reaction because many, if not most, students will try to get out of as much work as they can. However, when it comes from ethnic minority students, it is particularly irksome. This is partly because of the history of multiculturalism and how much people fought in the past for its inclusion in graduate training courses. Much of the impetus behind the pressure for its inclusion came from ethnic minority students' demands for courses that were personally meaningful to them, for a curriculum that reflected their own faces. Thus, when ethnic minority students want to opt out of these courses because they feel they have had some advanced undergraduate courses that have dealt with the same topic, it is not only disappointing to me, it is also a demonstration of lack of respect for the history of this issue.

I have had two such encounters with ethnic minority students wanting to opt out of my multicultural course. Both were from the same undergraduate program, and both had taken an advanced undergraduate course from one of the truly respected writers in the field. I have no doubt that these students received excellent information from this instructor, and because they knew that I knew this instructor, it was very difficult for me to deny these students' requests. The irksome thing about this situation was that two other ethnic minority students from the same undergraduate program also had taken a course with my colleague, yet they were so enthused about the area that they wanted to take my course too, and both felt they gained immeasurably from the course.

Upon reflection, I see that I should have not allowed the students to opt out of my course. I had a reputation in my department as being a very thorough and demanding professor, and I am certain that that was the reason they did not want to take my course. Moreover, they were older, more mature students by the time they would have taken my course, and they were also seeing clients, so the material would have been much more meaningful for them. When I teach my undergraduate course, I stick to general issues of multiculturalism or to specific issues encountered by specific ethnic minority groups. However, I do not take a clinical or interventional approach to the course, opting to save such issues for my graduate courses. Again, I have no doubt that these students received a fine education from my colleague. But this education may not have been as relevant to their clinical training as my graduate course would have been. I have to acknowledge that my own countertransference issues may have greatly influenced me, as I was a relative newcomer in the area of multiculturalism, whereas this colleague was an established name in the area. My own feelings of insecurity prevented me from taking a firmer stand on the issue. Once again, confessions of an author come to surface. With years and experience as my teachers, I will now discuss how the topics covered in their undergraduate course would be more directly relevant now that they were at the graduate level and conducting therapy sessions.

☐ Conclusions

With the requirement that all graduate students in the mental health professions be exposed to multicultural issues comes a subset of students who are resistant to such exposure. Today's instructors of multicultural courses must be prepared to address such resistance in a manner that respects the integrity of all students while remaining firm on the importance of multicultural awareness. Personally, I have found the identity development models to be effective in addressing some of this resistance. I also require weekly reaction papers so that students and I can have a private dialogue surrounding these issues. In this format, students are able to express what otherwise might be considered unpopular opinions in an atmosphere of safety. Other experiences, such as my game show exercise, can add an element of fun to the learning process. Sometimes issues of race and racism get weighty, and a bit of levity can reenergize student learning.

☐ References

Allport, G. W. (1954). *The nature of prejudice*. Reading, MA: Addison-Wesley.

Clavell, J. (1975). *Shogun*. New York: Dell.

Comas-Díaz, L., & Jacobson, F. M. (1991). Ethnocultural transference and countertransference in the therapeutic dyad. *American Journal of Orthopsychiatry, 61,* 392–402.

Cook, S. W. (1984). Cooperative interaction in multiethnic contexts. In N. Miller & M. Brewer (Eds.), *Groups in contact: The psychology of desegregation* (pp. 155–185). New York: Academic Press.

Cook, S. W. (1985). Experimenting on social issues: The case of school desegregation. *American Psychologist, 40,* 452–460.

Corvin, S., & Wiggins, F. (1989). An antiracism training model for White professionals. *Journal of Multicultural Counseling and Development, 17,* 105–114.

Cross, W. E., Jr. (1971). The Negro-to-Black conversion experience: Toward a psychology of Black liberation. *Black World, 20,* 13–27.

Hall, C. C. I. (1980). *The ethnic identity of racially mixed people: A study of Black–Japanese*. Unpublished doctoral dissertation, University of California, Los Angeles.

Helms, J. E. (1990). *Black and White racial identity: Theory, research and practice*. Westport, CT: Greenwood.

Jackson, L. C. (1996, August). Teaching diversity in clinical programs: Resistance and students of color. In J. S. Mio (Chair), *Institutional and individual resistances to multicultural issues—discussions and interventions*. Symposium presented at the 104th annual convention of the American Psychological Association, Toronto, Canada.

Mio, J. S. (1989). Experiential involvement as an adjunct to teaching cultural sensitivity. *Journal of Multicultural Counseling and Development, 17,* 38–46.

Parham, T. A. (1989). Cycles of psychological nigrescence. *The Counseling Psychologist, 17,* 187–226.

Pettigrew, T. F. (1981). Extending the stereotype concept. In D. L. Hamilton (Ed.), *Cognitive process in stereotyping and intergroup behavior* (pp. 303–331). Hillsdale, NJ: Erlbaum.

Ponterotto, J. G. (1988). Racial consciousness development among White counselor trainees: A stage model. *Journal of Multicultural Counseling and Development, 16,* 146–156.

Poston, W. S. C. (1990). The biracial identity development model: A needed addition. *Journal of Counseling & Development, 69,* 152–155

Sue, D. W., & Sue, D. (1990). *Counseling the culturally different: Theory and practice* (2nd ed.). New York: Wiley.

Thomas, K. W. (1976). Conflict and conflict management. In M. Dunnette (Ed.), *Handbook of industrial and organizational psychology* (pp. 889–936). Chicago: Rand-McNally.

Thomas, K. W. (1992). Conflict and negotiation processes in organizations. In M. D. Dunnette & L. M. Hough (Eds.), *Handbook of industrial and organizational psychology* (2nd ed., Vol. 3, pp. 651–717). Palo Alto, CA: Consulting Psychologists Press.

Triandis, H. C. (1989). The self and social behavior in differing cultural contexts. *Psychological Review, 96,* 506–520.

Triandis, H. C. (1995). *Individualism & collectivism.* Boulder, CO: Westview.

White, J. L. (1972). Towards a Black psychology. In R. C. Jones (Ed.), *Black psychology* (pp. 43–50). New York: Harper & Row.

CHAPTER **7**

Lori Barker-Hackett
and Jeffery Scott Mio

Addressing Resistance in Large Groups

Resistance to multicultural issues occurs in large groups for many of the same reasons described in preceding chapters for small groups, including naiveté, covert racism, and even overt racism. Nevertheless, there are dynamics unique to the large group setting that warrant attention, and a book like this would not be complete if it did not consider techniques for addressing and managing resistance in a large group. In this chapter the authors draw upon their experiences of encountering resistance in larger groups to discuss some of the causes of this resistance and some methods for managing it.

Multicultural training (or cross-cultural or diversity training, as it is sometimes called) has become very popular in many circles, from private corporations to government agencies to primary and secondary schools. These training sessions take on a wide variety of formats, from 2-hour workshops to week-long retreats, and are led by individuals with various levels of experience and expertise. Academicians—multicultural experts in particular—are being called upon more and more to apply their expertise to these issues outside of the classroom setting. We hope that the lessons we have learned from our own experiences will be helpful for others called upon to do this type of work. For further information, an excellent sourcebook is Theodore Singelis' recent publication, *Teaching about Culture, Ethnicity, & Diversity* (Singelis, 1998).

☐ Racial Identity Development Models

As discussed in the last chapter, racial identity development models seem to work in the classroom. We have found these models to work in larger groups as well, although because one cannot monitor reactions from participants as well in such a setting, it is best if one quickly presents these models, then has the audience break up into groups of 8 to 10 people to discuss how the models apply to their lives. Also, one of us (JSM) wrote the culture tale in Chapter 6 about the boy and his grandfather and developed it into a video. It makes a wonderful springboard into discussions of one's own culture tales and how they relate to one's racial identity. This tale has also been developed into a children's book adorned with illustrations by the mother of the author (Mio & Mio, under review). Most multicultural experts who have seen the finished product agree that the story has deep meaning, and it is difficult to deny its relevance to racial identity.

As an adjunct to the discussion of racial identity, we highly recommend the film *Color of Fear*, distributed by Lee Mun Wah (1993). This is a film about a weekend retreat involving eight men plus Lee—two African Americans, two Latino Americans, two Asian Americans, and two White Americans. All of the men except one White American, David Christianson, are aware of issues of racism and multiculturalism. The essence of the film is that the aware men expend a great deal of effort to break through David's resistance to multicultural issues and his denial that racism even exists. Instead, he feels that ethnic minorities bring racism on themselves because they see it in places where it does not exist. Finally, the men lead David to understanding, and he is able to see the importance of the issue. One reason David is able to achieve this breakthrough is that the men have an entire weekend of intensive group interactions devoted to working on multicultural issues. There is enough time for them to move through the various stages—getting acquainted, building tension, confronting emotions, and working through those emotions. Through them, we are able to see the entire process that leads to positive growth and change in David and the other members of the group.

☐ "A Class Divided"

A particularly powerful and effective videotape to show people is "A Class Divided," a Public Television program from the *Frontline* series (Peters, 1985). In this program, Jane Elliott's famous film, *Eye of the Storm*, is shown to the students who had been in her class 15 years earlier during her original demonstration. These former students then had the opportunity to discuss the ways in which her demonstration had changed their lives for the better. As many know, *Eye of the Storm* divided students into two groups, blue-eyed children and brown-eyed children. One day, the blue-eyed children were led to believe that all people with blue eyes were superior to those with brown eyes, and the next day, the brown-eyed children were led to believe the opposite was true. This is a particularly effective film that depicts how quick children are to assume a role of superiority. However, could this possibly happen to adults?

After *Eye of the Storm* and the ensuing discussion were shown, the program then moved on to demonstrate how Elliott has applied her basic idea to groups of adults. She has divided adults into groups of blue-eyed and brown-eyed individuals, having the brown-eyed individuals be the advantaged group. While the blue-eyed group has to wait for 45 minutes out in the hallway, the brown-eyed group is given instructions to play along with the premise of the exercise. Jane Elliott is a great actor in the film, spitting out contempt for the blue-eyed individuals and getting them to rebel, be meek, perform poorly, and so forth. In the follow-up discussion, many in the blue-eyed group said that even though they knew they were in an exercise that did not have any bearing on their job evaluations, personal lives, or other elements of life, they could not keep themselves from feeling swept up by the circumstances. Elliott asked one of the most obstreperous blue-eyed individuals if he was surprised at how he felt after only an hour and a half of a demonstration, and he said, "I was surprised at how I felt after only a few minutes!"

If one could pull it off, one could conduct such an exercise oneself. However, most cannot be as effective an actor as Jane Elliott, so we have resigned ourselves to merely showing this program and leading a discussion. The ensuing discussion always brings out the amazement audiences feel at how quickly and easily the blue-eyed individuals "fell victim" to Elliott's exercise. They also acknowledge the film's power in demonstrating the essential points of discrimination.

We always direct attention to a subtlety in the film of which Jane Elliott was not aware. As Lee Ross (1977) would say, she fell victim to the "fundamental attribution error" (see the discussion of this phenomenon in Chapter 4). At one point in the film, Ms. Elliott turns to one of her returning students and says, "Raymond, why were you so quick to discriminate against the other kids? When I went home that night, I thought, 'That miserable little Nazi!'" We point out to our audiences that Ms. Elliott had set up a context in which discrimination against those considered to be "inferior" was encouraged, and

Raymond complied by discriminating; then Ms. Elliott blamed a personality aspect in him for discriminating. In our society, we remove jobs and hope from inner cities, then we blame those in the inner cities for not pulling themselves up by their own bootstraps or for engaging in senseless violence in response to the senseless circumstances in which they find themselves.

☐ Experiential Exercises

The most popular method of addressing multicultural issues in a large group is the use of experiential exercises. These exercises typically are designed to evoke emotional responses in participants, facilitate interaction among group members from various backgrounds, and dramatize a particular multicultural issue. Although the intent of these exercises is to break through defenses and barriers that may exist among members of various groups, in and of themselves, they can engender resistance from participants.

Most of the authors' experience with large group exercises comes from our work with the annual Cross-Cultural Retreat sponsored by our campus, the California State Polytechnic University, Pomona (Cal Poly Pomona). The Cross-Cultural Retreat is held every year on one weekend in January. Participants are Cal Poly Pomona students, staff, and faculty. The average attendance is about 150 people, although in recent years, close to 200 individuals have wanted to participate in the event. This retreat has a 12-year history and has won awards as an exemplary program.

Target–Nontarget Groups

An exercise conducted quite often at the retreat is the Target–Nontarget exercise. In this exercise, first, people gather in the center of the room. One side of the room is labeled Target and the opposing side Nontarget. People are asked to move from the center to one side or the other, depending upon the classification into which they fall. The facilitator identifies the group. If you fall into that group, you are to move to the Target side of the room; if you do not, you move to the Nontarget side. For example, the moderator might say "women." If you are a woman you go to the Target side, and if you are a man, you go to the Nontarget side. After that, the group is asked to move back to the center of the room. The moderator then announces another category and members are again to move to the appropriate side. The list of categories varies and may include sexual orientation, age, coming from alcoholic families, individuals with disabilities, and so forth. The exercise is to be done silently, with only the moderator speaking. The participant's responsibility is to think about his or her own choice and to look at the people on the opposite side of the room and observe them. The essence of this exercise is to reinforce the notion that we all belong to groups that can become targets, depending upon the circumstances.

The authors have seen this exercise produce mixed results. It requires people to take risks they may not be prepared to take. A particularly sensitive issue is sexual orientation. Many people who have not come out find this exercise extremely difficult. If they go to the Target side of the room, they are acknowledging something about themselves they are not prepared to reveal; if they go to the Nontarget side of the room, they are denying something they know to be true and feel that they are lying to the entire audience. In the small group discussions following this exercise, one of the authors (JSM) has heard some lesbian and gay individuals discuss how offended they felt when they were on the Target side of the room. They felt there seemed to be a lot of curiosity on the Nontarget side of the room, as measured by the craning necks and tip-toed stares. Those who identified themselves as bisexual were also offended because they felt they had been left out of the exercise. Thus, another drawback of this exercise is that no matter how hard one tries, one risks missing a group and offending people who identify with that group.

Another memorable response in a small group discussion after a Target–Nontarget exercise was that of a woman reacting to the request that those who were from alcoholic families be the targets of observation. She spat out, "When I looked across the room at all of the Nontargets, my response was 'Liars!'" She came from an alcoholic family, and she felt that everyone came from alcoholic families and that those who remained on the Nontarget side of the room were simply denying the alcoholism in their families. This illustrates how emotionally evocative and potentially negative this exercise can be. Experiences like this can lead group members to resist participating in such activities in the future. However, some people have used this exercise to great effect and report that participants have been quite moved by it.

The Four Corners Exercise

A variation of the Target–Nontarget exercise is the Four Corners exercise. Here, signs are posted in the four corners of a room. The labels on these signs may vary, depending on the issues that are the focus of the retreat. For example, Gender/Sexual Orientation, Class/Socioeconomic Status/Education Level, Race/Ethnicity, and Faith/Religion/Spirituality were used at a recent Cross-Cultural Retreat. As in the Target–Nontarget exercise, participants stand in the center of the room. The moderator reads a question or phrase, and group members move to the appropriate corner of the room to answer the question or complete the phrase. The moderator usually begins with fairly easy questions, and the issues get more sensitive as the exercise progresses. Questions might be "This was most emphasized in the home I grew up in" or "This is my least favorite subject to talk about." Given that all of the corners have multiple possibilities (for example, Gender *or* Sexual Orientation), gravitation to that corner does not necessarily identify the participant with a specific topic or group. Moreover, because there are four potential groups, there is less of a tendency for people to look to see who is in the other groups. In fact, there is more of a tendency for people to look at those who have chosen the same group and to become more interpersonally connected with these like-minded individuals. On occasion, the moderator asks participants to talk with one another about why they have chosen that particular corner for the statement at hand, but by and large, this exercise is a silent one.

Some people find this exercise less threatening than the Target–Nontarget exercise, but it, too, requires participants to take some risks and perhaps admit to themselves things that they have not recognized before. Strong negative reactions have been observed in this exercise as well. For example, when this exercise was done at one of the Cross-Cultural Retreats with racial group labels in the four corners of the room, a few participants sat down in the middle of the room and refused to go to any corner. They were encouraged by the moderators to make a choice, but they adamantly refused. When asked why, they said they felt insulted and angered that they were being asked to make such choices. This was a very overt expression of resistance. In the debriefing session following this exercise, other participants said they were offended because their group was not represented, such as Middle Easterners and Africans who felt that the "Black/African American" label did not accurately describe them. In addition, some members were offended when they saw friends in other groups. For example, a European American participant was hurt when he saw his African American friend answer the question "What group would you least want to be?" by standing in the White/European American corner. In addition, he was frustrated because the exercise was silent and did not allow him to go to his friend and ask him why he was in that corner.

The Horatio Alger Exercise

One of the most meaningful large-group exercises in which we have ever participated was called the Horatio Alger Exercise (Empower Perspectives, ca. 1994). This exercise starts off with the moderator's explaining who Horatio Alger was and how Alger had stated that anyone could do whatever he or she wanted, that all it took was determination and one's own abilities.

The moderator assembles everyone in the center of a very large room, holding hands with the person on either side and forming a straight line. The moderator then reads a series of conditions and statistics, and each participant in the group described is to take a step or two forward or backward. For example, the moderator might describe the disparity between median White incomes and median ethnic minority incomes, and then ask all White participants to take two steps forward. Other statements might include the following: If your parents went to college, take one step forward. If a family member has ever been arrested, take one step backward. If you have ever been arrested, take two steps backward. If you live in an area where drugs are sold, take two steps backward. If you had a library card when you were a child, take one step forward.

It is quite dramatic to observe what happens when two people who have started off in the middle of the room holding hands have to give up their hand embrace because the distance between them has become too great. We have seen people stretch, with one foot on the floor and the other in the air, in an attempt to maintain fingertip contact until the next statement would force them to move even farther apart.

At the end of the exercise, people are to look around the room and notice who is at the front of the room and who is at the back of the room. Our first exposure to this exercise worked perfectly. For the most part, White males were pressed against the front wall, whereas many ethnic minorities were against the back wall. The ethnic minorities who were privileged were near the center of the room, and the Whites who were economically disadvantaged were also near the center of the room. Because of the built-in societal disadvantages for women, women tended to be in the back half of the room. The moderator's job at the end of this exercise is to repeat the philosophy Horatio Alger stood for and to point out that his words did not take into account the built-in societal advantages that some have. In addition, Horatio Alger did not take into account the built-in societal disadvantages confronting many.

The exercise is a very powerful and effective demonstration of these inequities. At the beginning of the exercise everyone starts out on a level playing field; by the end of the exercise, participants are scattered across the room. The visual distribution of ethnicities, genders, and economic circumstances is stunning. After this exercise was over, we discussed our thoughts and feelings about it, and the discussion was spirited. It is difficult to convey on paper the powerful effect this exercise had on us.

Although there is the potential for negative responses and resistance when using experiential exercises such as the ones described here, they can be used as opportunities for self-exploration, productive interaction, and positive change. Much of the responsibility for the effectiveness of such experiential exercises rests with the group facilitators and how they handle the emotional responses of the participants. These exercises are easy to implement, but it is not always easy to deal with the reactions they evoke. Unfortunately, many group facilitators feel that all they have to do is organize a couple of exercises and their job is done. In our opinion, the exercises are just the beginning. They are not an end in and of themselves but a tool that can be used to spark exploration and discussion. If handled improperly, they can leave participants with a bad taste in their mouths and lead to resistance. If handled properly, these exercises can help group members to increase self-understanding and develop empathy.

☐ Inclusion of Positive Experiences

One reason participants in large multicultural workshops may be resistant is that they have had bad experiences in such sessions in the past. For some group leaders, the main objective is to evoke emotions and foster confrontation, so they include exercises such as those previously described to accomplish these ends. Sometimes it seems as though they feel they are not successful as facilitators unless somebody gets angry, gets into an argument, or cries. In other instances, the focus may be entirely upon the negative aspects of intergroup relations, such as racism and discrimination, and on getting people to admit their racist ideas and tendencies. People then leave the workshop feeling angry, frustrated, embarrassed, and upset. The intention of these workshops is to improve relations; if people walk away with only negative experiences, they may further insulate themselves from others and may avoid such multicultural experiences in the future.

Expressions of emotion, arguments, and confrontations are not bad in and of themselves. Race is a highly emotional topic and we believe it is necessary to break down people's defenses to some degree in order for change to take place. However, this can be done in a constructive way that fosters positive growth or it can be done in a negative way that may actually make relations worse. Therefore, it is important to include opportunities for positive interactions when planning multi-cultural workshops.

The talent-sharing night we have every year at our Cross-Cultural Retreat is a good example of a positive group activity. Participants are encouraged to do anything they want to do. They read poetry, sing, dance, and do skits. Many of the acts involve sharing something unique to the individual's background or culture. For example, an African American student recited her favorite poem, "Phenomenal Woman" by Maya Angelou, and also choreographed her performance. Some of the staff and students from the Asian/Pacific Islander Student Center performed a rap song they wrote called "Diversity." Every year one of the authors (JSM) gets a group together to perform a song in sign language. Talent-sharing night is a time when people get to relax, laugh, and have a good time while celebrating the differences among them. This fosters positive bonding among group members and provides a nice contrast to the more difficult, intense activities of the weekend. Also, many students who plan to attend the retreat the next year work on their talent-sharing routines during the academic year, so the connection lasts far beyond the weekend of the retreat.

Another example of a positive activity that can be planned for a large group is a potluck, where each participant brings a dish typical of his or her particular culture. It might be a dish from the person's country of origin, something traditional from his or her own family, or simply a favorite recipe. Often there are stories that go along with each dish, and this provides another opportunity for group members to get to know one another and share with each other under more relaxed, informal, positive circumstances. People enjoy the food and the camaraderie. At a multicultural potluck one of the authors (LBH) attended recently, there were plantains from the West Indies, bratwurst from Poland, potato salad from Germany, hummus and pita bread from Lebanon, meatballs from Sweden, and sweet potato pie from Down South, to name just a few of the delicious dishes. Many conversations involved descriptions of the dishes and the cultural or family traditions behind them, and recipes were shared. (Not to mention that everyone ate until they could hold no more.)

Another example of a group exercise that fosters positive interactions is Favorite Things. There are a number of variations of this exercise. One is to type up a sheet with three columns. The first column is a list of favorites—favorite book, favorite movie, favorite food, favorite place, favorite color, and so forth. In the second column, participants fill in the items listed in the first column. That is, they fill in their own favorite movie, book, food, and so forth. Then they go around the room and find people who have the same favorites and that person signs his or her name in the appropriate place in the third column. In other words, if my favorite food is French fries, then I must go around the room until I find someone else whose favorite food is French fries, and that person signs his or her name next to French fries on my sheet, and vice versa. The winner is the first person to have a signature for every category. This activity also works as a good icebreaker because it is a way to get group members to mingle and meet one another. While they are mingling, they are also discovering the similarities and celebrating the differences among them.

A variation of the Favorite Things exercise is to put the categories on large pieces of butcher paper and tape them to the wall. The facilitator provides participants with multicolored markers and has them go around the room and write their favorite things on the pieces of paper. That way, the entire group can see each other's favorite things. Then they might be curious about the person who lists *Gone with the Wind* as his or her favorite movie and try to meet that person.

These are just a few examples of positive activities that can be included when facilitating large groups that are addressing multicultural issues. It is important to include opportunities for positive interaction so as to provide a balance for the necessary activities and exercises that evoke difficult and painful emotions and that may lead to confrontations and differences of opinion. However, if hard work is the only content of the workshop, people may leave feeling it was a negative experience and may be reluctant to participate in the future. Inclusion, activities that are fun and allow relaxation help to counterbalance these negative reactions.

☐ Debriefing and Processing

It is important to help participants get in touch with their true feelings and clarify their thoughts and opinions about multicultural issues. Workshop facilitators have become very good at this part of the training, but many times they fall short when it comes to helping participants to process their thoughts and feelings, and helping them to understand what their responses mean, where they come from, and what to do with them. Participants need assistance in understanding the emotions that arise and in working through them. Participants also need help in learning to express their feelings, ideas, and opinions to one another in constructive rather than destructive ways. Ample time must be built into workshop schedules to allow for this kind of work. When enough time is allowed for participants to work through their emotional responses, positive growth and change can take place.

As discussed before, the film *Color of Fear* (Lee, 1993) depicted a breakthrough in understanding by one resistant individual, David. This breakthrough could not have occurred had the men in the film not had an entire weekend to engage in intensive discussion. Our understanding is that many issues were discussed off camera or were edited out of the film, but these issues were crucial in setting the groundwork for the breakthroughs seen in the film. The unity among the men at the film's end was possible because David had time to demonstrate to the other men the sincerity of his understanding.

The Cross-Cultural Retreat at the authors' campus provides another illustration of the importance of building in enough time for debriefing and processing in larger group formats. At the first two retreats LBH attended, she felt very frustrated. The entire weekend was packed with activity after activity, each focused on a different topic. For example, they did one exercise on race, one on gender issues, and then another on sexual orientation, with hardly a pause in between. Strong emotions were stirred up, but there was never enough time to fully process them. When the participants complained, they were told to talk with each other during breaks (which were few), over meals, or late at night before going to bed. It was exhausting and frustrating.

Members of the retreat planning committee took subsequent feedback to heart and over the years, positive changes have been made. For the past 2 years, the retreat has focused on one topic for the entire weekend. Last year it was socioeconomic status, and this year it was race. There were still lots of activities, but the schedule was balanced between large group exercises designed to evoke thoughts and feelings and discussions in small groups. Group discussions took place in various formats ranging from small, mixed groups to single-race or socioeconomic status (SES) groups to the community as a whole. The retreat facilitators were sensitive to the climate of the community and actively sought feedback from group leaders and community members, and if the community needed more discussion and debriefing time, it was arranged. This system worked better. Much more movement and progress were evident by the end of the weekend, and participants left feeling positive and motivated.

An illustration of the positive benefits of this format can be seen in the retreat that focused on race. On Saturday afternoon, the community as a whole joined in an activity called a Fishbowl, in which one representative of each racial group sat in the center of the room and they had a discussion while the audience observed and listened. At one point, the African American young man said he felt he had to work harder than others to achieve the same goals and get the same recognition. This angered the representatives of the other groups who then felt they had to prove that they worked just as hard if not harder than the African American young man did. Members of the audience observing this interaction also began to get angry and make comments. Emotions were running high.

Immediately after that activity, we broke into single-race discussion groups—that is, all the African Americans together, all the Latinos together, and so forth. These groups were given about an hour to debrief the Fishbowl. Heated discussions took place in these groups and lively conversations continued during the break and over dinner. Based on observations of the group and feedback from group members, the facilitators changed the schedule and decided to have a community meeting after dinner. This allowed the entire group to further process what had taken place. After that, mixed-race groups discussed the activity again.

This might seem like overkill, but it illustrates the benefits of having enough time to debrief and process an emotion-provoking activity. The exercise brought up important issues, highlighted critical differences in perceptions among the racial groups, and facilitated the honest expression of emotions. It was important that a significant amount of time be spent helping participants to further express their feelings, understand them, and work through them.

The events that took place in the African American group provide additional illustrations of the importance of processing emotions. The discussion that took place immediately after the exercise revealed a lot of anger and tension. At first there was finger-pointing at other racial groups and a lot of standard talk about racism and how oppressed African Americans are and how this was just another example. However, members of the group were also challenged to take a look at themselves and their own behavior and to see how they had not made much effort over the weekend to really mingle with people from different backgrounds but had stuck together with members of their own group. It was acknowledged that this was done for social support and comfort, but the group accepted the challenge to move out of their comfort zones and speak with others about what had happened in the earlier session. During dinner, several of the African American students sat and talked with students from other groups, and during the community meeting they separated and sat in different sections. At our wrap-up session on Sunday, many of the African American students expressed how good they felt that they had stretched themselves and talked with others and how much they had learned.

They said that they would go back to campus with a new perspective, greater confidence, and increased openness to others from different backgrounds. Isn't that what such weekends are supposed to achieve?

Multicultural training sessions have to include exercises, activities, and presentations that evoke emotions. Participants must be able to confront difficult and painful issues and constructively discuss their differences of opinion. However, it is not enough just to evoke emotions and engender confrontations. Ample time must be allowed for participants to process their thoughts and feelings and acknowledge their differences in order for positive growth and change to take place.

☐ Building Empathy

Another reason group members may resist dealing with multicultural issues is that they can see things only from their own perspectives. To counteract this kind of tunnel vision it is important to include activities and exercises that help group members develop empathy for one another. A personal experience of one of the authors (LBH) helps to illustrate this:

> While I was working at a community mental health center we had an all-day mandatory staff training on cultural diversity. The program consisted primarily of speakers from each of the main ethnic minority groups who presented the major issues facing that group. Naturally, much of the discussion focused on racism and discrimination. At the last session of the day, one of the few White men (he actually was from a European country) in the room raised his hand and in a very frustrated voice said, "I'm tired of sitting here feeling like the epitome of all evil. All we've done today is talk about problems, and I feel like I'm being blamed for all of them. I want to know, what is the solution? What can we do to make things better?" As I sat and listened to him, I felt myself getting upset. I raised my hand and said, "You know what? I'm glad you feel uncomfortable, because what you're feeling right now is just a taste of what I feel every day, so I don't want to do anything to make you feel better. It's not my job to make you feel comfortable. I want you to sit there and feel those feelings because that is the only way you are going to have any empathy for what I go through as a Black woman, or what some of your ethnic minority clients might be going through." After the meeting, several members of the staff, all fellow people of color, came and told me how much they appreciated what I had said. They had been feeling upset too, but hadn't known how to put their feelings into words.

Inevitably, there will be someone in a larger group, often a European American (White) individual, who at some point feels uncomfortable and expresses it. Along with the expression of discomfort usually comes a request for the leaders or members of the group to "do something." Such requests to do something can be viewed as a form of resistance. The person is likely to be experiencing some combination of negative emotions—guilt, anger, frustration, fear—and is looking for a way to get rid of those emotions. However, as shown in the scenario above, the experience of these feelings provides a prime opportunity for the individual to develop a sense of empathy. An effective group leader, instead of trying to find a quick solution or trying to make the person feel more at ease and comfortable, encourages the individual and the rest of the group to process those feelings, helps the individual to label and express the feelings, and helps the ethnic minority members of the group to share their feelings in response. Such interaction can go a long way in the development of empathy among group members.

Many exercises are designed to develop empathy, such as activities in which participants are to "become" a member of a different group. This kind of exercise is more likely to be tried in a classroom than in a large group, but it could be made a large-group exercise for a period of time.

In some sign language classes, one of the assignments requires students to go out into the community and pretend to be deaf for a day. They have to find ways of meeting their needs, like buying food in a grocery store, buying clothes in an apparel store, or filling the car with gasoline, without speaking. They must learn how to interact with people in ways that will allow their needs to be serviced. In so doing, the students get a sense of the barriers deaf individuals encounter and thus gain empathy for their circumstances.

One way to adapt this exercise for a large group is to divide it into groups of a manageable size (8 to 10 participants each) and to assign participants to go to other groups to acquire a list of items. For example, they might want to buy opera tickets, find a certain brand of diapers, or get directions to a specific location fairly far away. Each group takes a turn at doing this, and then all gather for a discussion of the experience. This creates a sense of living in another's shoes and experiencing what deaf people have to go through on a daily basis.

Variations of this exercise include going around blindfolded for a day to experience what it is like to be blind, using a wheelchair for a day to experience what it is like to be physically challenged, and walking through a mall hand-in-hand with someone of the same sex to experience the social repercussions of being lesbian or gay. Such exercises provide little glimpses into the realities of others' lives that can help people understand other cultures and ways of life, and it should help them to transfer this knowledge to other multicultural issues.

The building of this type of empathy can go a long way toward breaking down resistance to multicultural issues.

☐ Balancing Emotional and Intellectual Aspects

Overemphasis on the emotional aspects of multicultural issues is often accompanied by the failure to provide a cognitive framework within which participants can also gain an intellectual understanding of the issues. In our experience, it is important to provide a balance between emotion and intellect. Exercises designed to evoke emotions can be counterweighted with didactic instruction during which participants can benefit from the extensive and expanding amount of literature in the area of multiculturalism.

For example, it is helpful to educate participants about the dynamics of culture, racism, prejudice, discrimination, and stereotypes. Many people do not even know the difference among these terms. It is helpful to provide accurate definitions and structure group discussions around them. For instance, as noted in Chapter 4, cognitive psychology has taught us that stereotypes may be a way by which our minds summarize, organize, and store vast amounts of information. Stereotypes are bad when we rely on them and insist on keeping them, even in the face of contradictory evidence. It is helpful for group members to learn the benefits of stereotyping so they can balance them with the costs.

Our friend Shelly Harrell developed a course in cross-cultural competence for the California School of Professional Psychology in Los Angeles. This course includes a module called Dealing with Difference. The goal is to help everyone to understand how we respond when we are in situations in which we feel different or in which we encounter people who are different from us. One of the authors (LBH) has successfully adapted this information for use in large groups.

There are four ways in which people who are resistant typically deal with difference. First, people have a tendency to deny differences or pretend that they are not there. Statements such as "We're all from the same race—the human race," and "We all bleed red," and "I don't see color" reflect the tendency to deny differences.

A second response people have is to distance themselves from the different person or situation. When people feel different or encounter others who are different, they feel uncomfortable, and one of their first inclinations is to get out of that situation and get back to a place where they feel more comfortable. Usually that is with others who are similar. For example, if a person at a party is the only one of a particular ethnicity in the room, he or she may decide to leave early. Another example can be seen in the research on early termination of therapy by ethnic minorities (e.g., Sue, 1977; Sue, Fujino, Hu, Takeuchi, & Zane, 1991; Sue & McKinney, 1974; Sue, McKinney, Allen, & Hall, 1974; Sue, Zane, & Young, 1994). A possible explanation for this phenomenon is that both therapist and client may be uncomfortable with the cultural differences and may therefore distance themselves from the situation by cutting therapy short.

There is also a tendency to devalue things and people that are different. Human beings, or at least those in this culture, tend to have a "difference equals deficiency" bias. In other words, anything that is different or strange is seen as being less good than things that are familiar. For example, one often hears comments such as, "Stupid [fill in the foreign group]. Why don't they learn to speak English?" The fact that an immigrant does not speak English does not automatically make that person less intelligent. Or we hear critics calling a foreign form of music or piece of artwork "primitive," "simple," or "basic." Just because it is unfamiliar, it is not automatically inferior, but somehow there seems to be a bias that makes people place something different in a hierarchy in relation to themselves and other familiar things. The bias leads people to place themselves on top and to place what is different in a lower position.

Finally, people may respond to difference by becoming defensive. Statements such as "I'm not a racist" and "Some of my best friends are Black" reflect defensiveness. Defensiveness is a common response, and not only for those who are uninformed regarding issues of race, culture, and ethnicity. It is also a response by individuals who pride themselves on being sensitive to multicultural issues when they find themselves in situations in which they feel uncomfortable or feel that their level of sensitivity being challenged.

If people become more aware of their tendencies to deny, distance, devalue, and become defensive (the "Ds of Difference"), they gain more control and can choose to do something else. Instead of being afraid or uncomfortable, they can take the opportunity to learn something new. Group members can be taught that dealing with difference is not all negative. Encountering people different from oneself provides an opportunity for a new D, discovery—discovery of people's different backgrounds, where they are from, what languages they speak, what kinds of things they like to do. People often tell us they are afraid to ask such questions because they might offend someone. That could happen, but more often people are glad someone cares enough to ask and are more than happy to share something about themselves. People can learn something new, broaden their own perspectives, break down the walls of mistrust and separation, and maybe even make new friends. Incidentally, the quickest way to turn off someone from a different culture is simply to ask, "What are you?" First of all, the question itself is off-putting. Second, quite often those who ask the question in this manner simply wait to hear the answer, then walk away. However, if they were to ask something like, "What is your ethnic background?" and engage in a conversation, then the seeds of friendship have been planted.

Teaching group members how people respond to difference can be quite helpful, but the next step is to take them through a group exercise that will bring the various points to life. First, group members are to think of a time when they felt different. They might write down what happened, along with the thoughts and feelings they had during that experience. Then they share their experiences. The group can break up into dyads or small groups (no larger than four to six members) and share their experiences, or volunteers can share with the group as a whole.

The didactic portion of this training in which participants are taught about the Ds of Difference gives people a cognitive understanding of why they do some of the things they do. The exercise in which they write down a personal experience of being different and share it with others helps them to connect with the experience emotionally and develop empathy for others from different backgrounds. All individuals have had some kind of experience of being different. If they can remember those experiences and the feelings and thoughts associated with them, then they can empathize with others and develop greater sensitivity to what it is like to be culturally different.

☐ Conclusions

Resistance is a natural part of group interactions and should be expected, especially when dealing with such an emotionally charged issue as multiculturalism. Therefore, it is important for those who are called upon to conduct workshops and seminars to have a variety of methods available for dealing with this resistance. In the authors' opinion, much of the resistance can be addressed, even circumvented, in the planning stages. Large group sessions should be designed to include didactic instruction, experiential exercises, small group discussions, large group discussions, and positive experiences. There should be a balance between the emotional and the intellectual aspects, and ample time should be allowed for debriefing and processing. Expressions of emotion and differences of opinion should be encouraged but should be handled in a respectful and constructive manner. Exercises should build empathy and encourage positive discovery among members. If these recommendations are followed, resistance is minimized and the chances for positive growth and change are increased.

These suggestions come from the authors' personal experiences leading and participating in multicultural workshops, seminars, and training sessions. We have described the methods we have found to be most effective. The next step is to conduct studies of the effectiveness of these methods. Most of the research on multicultural training has been done in graduate-level clinical and counseling psychology programs (e.g., D'Andrea, Daniels, & Heck, 1991; Neville, Heppner, Louie, Thompson, Brooks, & Baker, 1996; Pedersen, 1987; Pope-Davis, Reynolds, Dings, & Nielson, 1995; Sodowsky, 1996). However, because multicultural training has become so popular in other settings, such as corporations, government, and primary and secondary schools, more emphasis has to be placed on gathering empirical evidence about work with these groups. Future efforts should include research into which strategies are actually most effective in which settings, and with which populations. At this time, our intuitions about the effectiveness of the exercises and activities presented here remain strong; we would like to see data to back up our intuitions.

☐ References

D'Andrea, M., Daniels, J., & Heck, R. (1991). Evaluating the impact of multicultural training. *Journal of Counseling and Development, 70,* 143–150.

Empower Perspectives. (ca. 1994). *Horatio Alger exercise.* Los Angeles: Author.

Lee, M. W. (Producer and Director). (1994). *Color of fear* [Film]. (Available from Stir-Fry Productions, 1222 Preservation Park Way, Oakland, CA 94612)

Mio, J. S., & Mio, R. T. (under review). *The rice bowl.*

Neville, H., Heppner, M., Louie, E., Thompson, C., Brooks, L., & Baker, C. (1996). The impact of multicultural training on White racial identity attitudes and therapy competencies. *Professional Psychology: Research and Practice, 27,* 83–89.

Peters, W. (1985). A class divided. In D. Fanning (Producer), *Frontline.* Boston: WGBH.

Pope-Davis, D. B., Reynolds, A. L., Dings, J. G., & Nielson, D. (1995). Examining multicultural competencies of graduate students in psychology. *Professional Psychology: Research and Practice, 26,* 322–329.

Ross, L. D. (1977). The intuitive psychologist and his shortcomings: Distortions in the attribution process. In L. Berkowitz (Ed.), *Advances in experimental social psychology* (Vol. 10, pp. 173–220). New York: Academic Press.

Singelis, T. M. (Ed.). (1998). *Teaching about culture, ethnicity, & diversity.* Thousand Oaks, CA: Sage.

Sodowsky, G. R. (1996). The Multicultural Counseling Inventory: Validity and applications in multicultural training. In G. R. Sodowsky & J. C. Impara (Eds.), *Multicultural assessment in counseling and clinical psychology* (pp. 283–324). Lincoln, NE: Buros Institute of Mental Measurements.

Sue, S. (1977). Community mental health services to minority groups: Some optimism, some pessimism. *American Psychologist, 32,* 616–624.

Sue, S., Fujino, D. C., Hu, L., Takeuchi, D. T., & Zane, N. W. S. (1991). Community mental health services for ethnic minority groups: A test of the cultural responsiveness hypothesis. *Journal of Consulting and Clinical Psychology, 59,* 533–540.

Sue, S., & McKinney, H. (1975). Asian Americans in the community mental health care system. *American Journal of Orthopsychiatry, 45,* 111–118.

Sue, S., McKinney, H., Allen, D., & Hall, J. (1974). Delivery of community health services to Black & White clients. *Journal of Consulting Psychology, 42,* 794–801.

Sue, S., Zane, N., & Young, K. (1994). Research on psychotherapy with culturally diverse populations. In A. E. Bergin & S. L. Garfield (Eds.), *Handbook of psychotherapy and behavior change* (4th ed., pp. 783–820). New York: Wiley.

Resistance at the Administrative Level

As an administrator, I (GIA) see resistance to multiculturalism on many levels, including administration, faculty, staff, and students. This chapter examines resistance on all of these levels as observed through the eyes of Gene I. Awakuni and is written in part by Jeffery Scott Mio. We also address resistances to multiculturalism that administrators, even the most committed ones, may be unintentionally succumbing to. In so doing, we hope to give the reader a sense of what it is like to be an administrator who is himself of an ethnic minority group and who ""is trying to advance the cause of multiculturalism on an ethnically diverse campus.

In many respects, this university is quite different from most other universities. Not only is the president of the university, Bob H. Suzuki, an ethnic minority administrator himself; with the resignation of Chancellor Chang-Lin Tien of the University of California, Berkeley, he is one of only three Asian presidents or chancellors of a major university in the country. As noted in Chapter 3, Dr. Suzuki is personally committed to the ideals of diversity and multiculturalism. His commitment, however, is perceived to be coercive pressuring of others to accept multiculturalism. These attempts have been resisted by challenges presented to him on a number of seemingly unrelated issues. Some of these issues were already discussed in Chapter 3, but for the purposes of this chapter, we will discuss them in more formal categories.

☐ Vision

Many on campus have questioned President Suzuki about his vision of the future. Because vision is teleological, it cannot be affirmed or disconfirmed in the present. Thus, such criticisms may be made without fear of contradiction. One may agree or disagree with the vision of an individual, but one cannot prove that one's vision is correct or incorrect. Similarly, criticisms of vision cannot be proven correct or incorrect; all one has to do is to develop a critical mass of vocal critics, and paralysis can ensue. Resistance is the goal; paralysis is success.

☐ Demonstration of Power

Some may resist by discounting an administrator's policies, framing them as mere power plays or demonstrations of power. Thus, they are questioning the sincerity of the administrator's commitment to a goal by conceptualizing it as merely a game. The substance of the debate is irrelevant; winning and losing is everything. Resisters may thus keep score and remember how many times they have "won" versus how many times the administrators have "won."

One quite often hears comments like, "Oh, this will blow over, and another issue will take its place." In conceptualizing every issue in this manner, truly important issues like multiculturalism are minimized. If resistance can be kept up long enough, there will no longer be any demands to diversify one's department or one's way of thinking.

☐ Responding to External Forces

Resisters also have success in minimizing truly important issues such as multiculturalism by framing them not as a game or power play but as a response to external forces, such as the college's governing board or the state legislature or legal concerns. Again, this allows resisters to discount the importance of the issue to the administrator. If one does not feel that the administrator is sincere in his or her demands for multiculturalism, the issue is much easier to resist.

☐ Administrator-to-Administrator Relationships

Some administrators may resist the initiatives of other administrators who are different in race, class, or gender. The initiatives can be framed as being insensitive to the demographics of the other administrators.

This is a particularly effective form of resistance to the issue of multiculturalism, for an oft-used synonym of "multiculturalism" is "diversity." If you are truly committed to issues of diversity, and if someone of a different demographic group from yourself criticizes you for being insensitive to his or her group, your instincts may be to back down and proceed more slowly. This gives the power to the resister, and the resistance can be stretched out for a longer period of time.

☐ Ascribed Versus Earned Credibility

Sue and Zane (1987) proposed a model of multiculturalism that describes two levels of ascribed credibility and two levels of earned credibility. In dealing with ethnic minority clients, ethnic minority therapists have an advantage over their nonethnic minority counterparts because they are ascribed high credibility in their ability to understand ethnic minority issues. Nonethnic minority therapists do not have this ascribed credibility. This initial ascription of credibility to the ethnic minority therapist is unearned. Over time, however, the ethnic minority therapist must earn credibility in order for the ethnic minority client to maintain trust; the nonethnic minority therapist may have a chance to earn this credibility, too. Obviously, both the ethnic minority and the nonethnic minority therapists may lose credibility, leading to termination of therapy or at least a negative therapeutic result.

When a nonethnic minority administrator advocates for multicultural concerns, he or she may experience resistance because of lack of credibility. However, ethnic minority administrators, like those on our campus, may run into a different set of problems, as their commitments to multicultural concerns may be discounted because of "mere" ascription of credibility. Because of this form of resistance, the administrator may never be given the chance to earn credibility on the issue ("Oh, he's just doing this because he is Asian.").

Overall, administrators can push their commitment to multiculturalism through varying forms of "carrots" and "sticks." If they are truly committed to this issue, they can be effective by maintaining a consistent message, offering rewards for adherence to multiculturalism, and judiciously using pressure in this area.

☐ Administrative Cases

It is possible to cite many examples of cases in which ethnic minority leaders have had to cope with resistance to their presence in the administration. Even administrators who embrace a multicultural philosophy, at times may inadvertently or unconsciously contribute to the undermining of diversity efforts. The examples presented, informed by one of the authors' (GIA) experiences as an administrator, are not meant to be exhaustive but rather to illustrate the numerous ways in which efforts toward diversity can be derailed and thus indicate how enormously difficult it is to create a multicultural community.

(Fill in the Color) on the Outside, White on the Inside

When a minority administrator has been hired partially because of a lack of diversity in the institution, a tremendous burden is placed on the shoulders of that individual. Underrepresented constituent groups on campus view with great expectations the arrival of a new administrator who may represent their interests. In many instances, these groups have lobbied long and hard for representation in the administration so that their priorities would be addressed. It cannot be assumed, however, that the minority administrator has a commitment to further the diversity agenda on campus. There are many instances when a minority administrator's reference group orientation is more closely aligned with mainstream White culture than with his or her own ethnic group.

What does this have to do with resistance to cultural change? Plenty. In this case, that very individual may be an obstacle to change. A recent example of this in California is Ward Connerly, a Regent of the University of California, who led the successful statewide effort to overturn admission preferences for ethnic minorities. Mr. Connerly, an African American, repeatedly chose to ignore history and dispute the importance of affirmative action policies that have led directly to many minority group members' accessing education and special programs they would not otherwise have been able to take advantage of. Stories abound about individuals who have utilized opportunities provided by affirmative action programs to achieve success as doctors, lawyers, captains of industry, teachers, and so forth.

Don't Mind Me, I Don't Exist

Most minority administrators I have talked with over the past few years can relate at least one story and usually many regarding the invisibility with which they must often deal. Sometimes the behavior is subtle and sometimes it is blatantly obvious. In either case, it sends a strong message that the minority administrator's opinion is not valued as much as that of a White administrator's. For example, at the previous university at which I worked, I served on the president's executive council along with all the other senior administrators. It was a group composed of 20 people who met on a biweekly basis. Of these 20 administrators, 2 were Asian American, 2 Latino, and 1 African American. After the first couple of times I attended those meetings, I realized that the other Asian American administrator, who happened to be the graduate dean and an internationally known linguist, never attended. I asked him why he had decided not to attend, and he responded that it was a big waste of time. He related an incident that had occurred during a meeting he had attended a few months earlier. At that meeting, the president had asked for feedback regarding an issue with which the dean was very familiar; in fact he had written quite extensively on the topic. As it turned out, he was not asked for his opinion on the matter. When he volunteered that he knew the subject matter and could provide some insight, his comment was very politely brushed aside. Other members of the group, taking their cue from the president, who had ignored him completely, continued their conversation as if he had not uttered a word. This administrator appeared to be facing the difficult task, indeed the challenge, of convincing his White male colleagues (the group happened to be all male) that he spoke with knowledge and authority. Because of his physical appearance (he is thin and his weak eyesight requires thick wire-rimmed glasses) and his heavy accent, it seemed that people had trouble viewing him as credible. The other ethnic administrators who were at the meeting, because of their unwillingness to be similarly treated, did nothing to defend him publicly. But privately they commiserated with him and expressed to him that they often felt the same way.

You're an Exception to the Rule

When I first began my career as a senior administrator, I was told by an African American colleague that I would not establish credibility with my administrator peers until I made a tough decision. This is something that all administrators have to deal with, but it was compounded because of my ethnicity. The impression was that my being Asian American meant that I didn't have the ability to be decisive and firm. A couple of months after my arrival on campus, in my new position as an assistant vice chancellor, I had to fire a very popular senior manager. He was a White male who had established himself by being a major player in campus politics and as the president of an influential national association. The decision to terminate this manager was simply the culmination of a year-long investigation in which he was implicated in major impropriety. Hence, although I was merely the administrator in charge when the decision to terminate was made, because of confidentiality laws, the campus community had little information about the events leading up to the termination.

My reputation as an administrator with the courage to make a difficult decision grew from that experience and I found myself thereafter being called upon to take on assignments that required a tough-minded negotiator. My sense was, however, that the image of Asian American men had not changed in the minds of people on campus. I was often told that I was unlike other Asian men. People tried to discern why and frequently concluded that it was my upbringing in Hawaii, where Asians happen to be in the majority, and my third-generation status that led to my assimilation of Western values and my ability to function well in a higher-education setting. So although I was viewed as credible, the stereotypes of Asians remained embedded in people's psyches. Their ability to establish an exception to the rule allowed people to pigeonhole my interpersonal style and behavior into a convenient category without disturbing their stereotypes of Asians as an ethnic group.

It's Lonely Up Here

When an individual is the only one of a particular racial group in the administration, isolation often occurs, with fairly predictable results. An African American colleague of mine who was the chief academic officer of a middlesized, comprehensive institution told me how difficult it was for him to feel that he belonged. Although people were cordial and respectful, he never got the sense that he was a part of the senior administrative team. He was certain that some of the senior administrators were meeting for drinks after work without him. And although he played golf regularly, he was never invited to play with the group of White male administrators who had a standing weekend tee time.

It is difficult to know whether this African American administrator was treated differently because of his skin color or because of other characteristics, especially his choice of clothing and accessories and his lack of social skills. His suits were not the standard colors and styles preferred by senior administrators at his campus, and the jewelry he wore (a gold bracelet and several large rings) seemed inappropriate for a senior-level representative of a very conservative institution. In addition, he did not have the social skills that many mainstream Americans expect in a leader. For instance, he was unable to make "cocktail party conversation" which made him seem painfully ill at ease at receptions and dinners. At the very least, this administrator's cultural values reinforced the racial difference and the social divide that his peers perceived.

Over time he became depressed and began to avoid interactions even with his staff, and he grew less and less communicative. People started describing him as being aloof and inaccessible. This characterization led people to conclude that he had difficulty relating to people and therefore would not be able to persuade faculty and others to embrace his vision. Primarily because of the lack of confidence the faculty had expressed in his leadership and because of his relative inability to establish meaningful relationships with staff and administrator colleagues, the president had very little choice but to ask him to step down from his position. The tragedy in the situation was that this administrator had some excellent ideas about how to build upon the core strength of the institution's fine academic programs. But people chose to focus on the differences that set him apart from themselves. Unfortunately for this administrator and many others in this predicament, there are no mentors who understand their cultural values and their plight and who could help them find ways of closing the social gap between themselves and others and overcome the isolation.

You're Not All the Same After All

As I mentioned earlier, the president of the university where I work is Asian American. When I arrived to assume the role of Vice President for Student Affairs, it was the first time that any 4-year institution had had two Asian American cabinet officers. I believe this is still the case. Both faculty and staff have told me that at first they were not sure what to expect from me, but that they now have a better appreciation of the diversity within the Asian American community. They have learned this because of what they have observed over the 6 years I have been on campus. The president is a product of his generation and I of mine. His stoic demeanor and formal style are reflective of a Japanese American born before World War II and raised during a time of bitter racism that targeted Japanese Americans. I, on the other hand, a baby boomer, was born at a time of prosperity in America and came of age in the '60s and '70s when sushi, Bruce Lee, and the Beatles were in vogue. My liberal values and informal interpersonal style have been an advantage in my efforts to establish relationships with people from various constituent groups on campus.

At first, people told me that I was fortunate because I had a special relationship with the president. Although it was usually unstated, this seemed to me to be a subtle way of saying that our common Asian heritage made it easier for the president and me to establish a bond. The underlying message suggests that I had an advantage over other administrators. In fact, frequently my colleagues would say, "Well, Gene, you have a good relationship with the president, so we'd like you to talk to him about such and such on our behalf." As it was, I had no special insight into the president's personality and no particular advantage over anyone else. I have done nothing to actively combat this mistaken impression that many people have held except to express my views as honestly as I can and to interact with people in a way that feels comfortable to me. This has led people to tear down the stereotypic images they had held of Asians and to realize that, like Whites, the president and I can be—and are—very different people whose personalities are almost at polar ends of the continuum.

Two's Company, Three's a Crowd

I joined an administration that at the time was composed of two Asian American (the president and myself), two African American, and two Euro-American members. The change in the composition of the executive leadership team had taken place quite dramatically after the arrival of the president 2 years before. Prior to his arrival, all but one of the senior administrators had been White.

Resistance to the initiatives put forth by the current leadership team, although not always overt, occurred regularly and reflected, I would submit, the campus community's inability to accept the radical change in the complexion of its senior administrators. Almost immediately upon his arrival, the president was characterized as being too intrusive, a micromanager who wanted to control faculty rather than allow them the freedom to prosper as teachers and scholars. This expression of resistance from faculty, I believe, was a backlash against the entire administration that began increasingly to look very different from what the faculty remembered during the "good old days."

It seems inevitable that a reaction from mainstream groups will occur when minority administrators on a particular campus reach a critical mass. A primary challenge to a cabinet such as the one described above is to maintain credibility with all constituent groups. The White majority who had seen its members dominate by holding prominent leadership positions sought ways to recreate the comfort and familiarity of the former composition of the campus leadership.

Their drive to achieve this end may not manifest itself as a conscious intention but rather may be more indicative of a subconscious desire to restore social equilibrium.

Cox (1994) describes the phenomenon that occurs when people from a particular racial and socioeconomic group are asked to rate the desirability of people from other groups: they choose people who look and act much like themselves. When applied to the setting I have just discussed, it is easy to see how the White majority might feel discomfort with and resentment toward the new administration. This can lead to harsh attacks regarding the president's judgment and ability to lead. For example, on our campus, the president's emphasis on creating linkages with global partners, especially in Asia, drew much criticism and cries of cronyism. The local press whipped up the controversy by chronicling what it alleged to be presidential improprieties, and the fire was fueled by the faculty's allegations that the president had misused his office by hiring a friend to lure Korean students to the campus's English Language Institute. The president was roundly criticized for his trips to Asia and for expending precious institutional resources during a time of budget austerity. Later, after an investigation by an outside auditor, the president was totally exonerated from any wrongdoing. The English Language Institute, which the president had traveled to Asia to promote, has proven to be a financial gold mine, generating thousands of dollars of revenue for the campus. This revenue is being used to strengthen academic programs.

I provide this example to illustrate how easily accusations can be made by opponents and accepted by the general public because of prevailing societal stereotypes. Whether it was done intentionally or not, the cultural heritage of the president was unfairly portrayed to depict him in such a way as to conjure up in the public's mind the specter of a foreigner who is taking advantage of his position and of our American way of life.

In addition, underrepresented constituent groups who do not have representation on the senior leadership team will continue to press for representation and may resist the efforts of the administration to establish diversity programs without first ensuring that their needs are met. In the situation described above, there were no administrators who were Latino. This was a problem that the Latino faculty, staff, and students believed needed to be redressed immediately, and they put their demand in a memorandum that was sent to the president and the members of the cabinet. In response to the Latino community and to try to engender greater recognition of the need to create a campus community that embraces diversity, the president established a cabinet-level position for Diversity and Affirmative Action Compliance. The first person hired for that position was a highly respected Latina scholar from another campus. In the 2 years she spent in the position, she was able to establish strong ties to members of the Latino community. This led directly to greater support from that constituent group for the president's initiatives.

Let's Move Diversity to the Second Tier on the Priority List

In my experience as an administrator, especially during times of crisis, I have observed that it has been very easy and convenient to put aside efforts aimed at changing the campus culture and diversifying the institution. In the daily life of an institution, issues invariably arise that require immediate attention, such as a budget shortfall, faculty unrest, and the like. Cultural change and diversity seem too abstract for many people to grasp fully. Does it mean hiring more minorities? Or does it mean embracing a new philosophy? If so, what is it and what are the implications of operationalizing it? Will it impact what I do as a faculty member, staff, or student? These are questions that have no simple or definitive answers and thus create a sense of uncertainty that most people, including administrators, would prefer not to have to contend with.

Thus, even those who are most committed to changing the campus culture may find it difficult to muster the will to stay the course in the face of competing demands for time and resources. I can recall several occasions on which the topic of diversity was scheduled to be discussed at a cabinet meeting only to be moved to a later date in the term or the year because of the need to discuss other pressing matters. Most of the time, the diversity issue, when it reappeared, was never given the serious consideration necessary to ensure that a viable institution-wide plan could be adopted and implemented. Often this deferral of diversity to second-tier priority was not even recognized by those who believed they were simply dealing with the essential requirements of running a complex institution of higher learning rather than realizing that they were dealing with their own lack of will to carry forward the cultural diversity agenda.

In addition, the task of changing a campus culture is so daunting that frequently even well-intentioned administrators have very little hope that any effort can be successful. This skepticism may lead prudent administrators to eschew the commitment of significant resources, fearing that the funds expended would be wasted on a costly and futile attempt to achieve an admirable but unattainable goal.

We're Reinventing the Wheel

One of the most frustrating experiences for administrators who have spent a great deal of time and energy on diversity projects occurs when nothing is ever done to follow up on a successful initiative. To add insult to injury, another initiative may later emerge that is not connected to the successful one that preceded it but bears a striking resemblance to the prior project. Moreover, many of the programs appear very similar to initiatives that first gained popularity years ago. As an illustration, our campus decided to participate in a national teleconference on race sponsored by the White House. It was intended to be a campus–community collaboration that would allow civic and political leaders, business executives, faculty, students, and administrators the opportunity to engage in dialogue with each other about race relations and to come up with ways of closing the social distances among groups. And it was hoped, as well, that solutions would be generated that would address society's most vexing social problems.

The dialogue session ended with heated exchanges about the lack of progress in the area of sociocultural change. Many people who participated left the conference feeling as if we were no further ahead than we were 20 years ago. The strides made during the civil rights struggles in the 1960s have in their minds gradually eroded. One community leader told me that it seemed to her that she was back in the mid '70s. The solutions proposed appeared to be almost identical to the ones we have been trying to implement for quite some time, like improving access to education and creating more adjunctive and school-to-work programs. Similarly, on campus, often purportedly "new" diversity initiatives appear to be a recycling of old ideas such as awareness-training seminars, curriculum infusion, and the like.

When new-old initiatives are proposed, the "here we go again" attitude rears itself, and passive resistance usually follows. That is to say, an administrator may go through the motions of carrying out a diversity plan but not feel a strong commitment toward it, which can very quickly lead to the plan's failure and to mounting frustration in the campus community.

You're Insulting My Intelligence, I Know What to Do

I have frequently encountered administrators who tell me, "Look Gene, I may not be a minority person but I do know how to treat people with respect, so tell the president and the members of the cabinet to let me implement a diversity plan my way." Their resistance is not to the notion of embracing cultural diversity per se but rather to the coercion they feel is applied by the president or cabinet-level officers. This is a difficult issue to address because any effort to show such administrators that they may be much better off following the direction established by the president may hit those administrators where they are most heavily defended. "What do you mean, I don't understand the plight of underrepresented people? I do, but I don't see the need for any special treatment for those groups." Many administrators have good intentions but may harbor deeply rooted biases of which they are completely unaware against certain constituent groups. When attempts are made to point out the inconsistencies in what these administrators say and actually do, it can arouse in them passionate defense of their behavior. "I am as committed to fairness and equity as anyone in the university" is often the reply from administrators whose commitment to diversity has been challenged.

To further reinforce such administrators' resistance, they are usually expected to indicate during their annual performance reviews what they have done to further the campus diversity plan. At our institution, this makes up 20% of administrators' work. I have heard enough comments from disgruntled administrators to believe that the mandated nature of this expectation causes some individuals to become resentful about what they are required to do to ensure they receive a favorable job review.

☐ Faculty

Many faculty members who are resistant to the ideals of multiculturalism may find ways of resisting that follow the lines of modern forms of racism discussed in Chapter 3. Faculty may be slow to change, may complain about "less prepared" students, and may indulge in stereotyping, and there may be only small numbers of committed faculty.

Slow to Change

Some professors are not inherently opposed to the ideals of multiculturalism; like the rest of us, they may simply have a fundamental resistance to change. For example, if one were asked to include aspects of diversity in a course in physiology, the professor might reason, "What does diversity have to do with physiology? We all have fundamentally the same physiological systems. Besides, I have crammed so much important information into my course that I cannot possibly include another topic without eliminating what I see as fundamental to my course." This, of course, ignores some real differences between males and females and how some substances or drugs may interact differently, depending upon the ethnicity of the individual—for example many Asians do not have the enzymes to break down milk and alcohol.

McIntosh (1986) discussed her own frustration when trying to convince her male colleagues to include in their courses issues involving women. She reported how these colleagues gave reasoned answers as to why such issues were not fundamental to their courses. Others mentioned that they would have to eliminate some important topics in their already existing sets of notes in order to include such literature (not to mention the time and effort it would take for them to become familiar with the new material). Ironically, McIntosh used the exact same arguments when some colleagues of color asked her to include issues involving race and ethnicity in her women's studies courses. It then hit her that she was being hypocritical, and she immediately included such topics in her courses. Her paper on the topic has been re-presented and reprinted in a variety of settings because of its power and fundamental truth.

Thus, some professors may not be personally resistant to multiculturalism, they may simply not see its importance to their particular area of study or may not be sufficiently motivated to incorporate it. We have discussed only inclusion in course material, but resistance does not have to be limited to that area. Across our campus, there are numerous opportunities for professors to be exposed to issues of diversity that would help them deal with the changing student body as they see it in their own classes, but time and again, we see the same faces in these sessions. Many of us are familiar with the terms "preaching to the choir" and "ghettoized sessions," as this has been the complaint about sessions dealing with diversity at major conferences. Those most in need of being exposed to such issues tend not to attend the sessions, and those who are most aware do attend.

Complaints about "Less Prepared" Students

Most of us are aware that the term "less prepared" students is a code phrase for "ethnic minority" students. Because of the changing demographics of the student body on today's campuses, many who are attending colleges and universities speak English as their second language. Questions asked in class are often more difficult to understand as a result of students' accented English, so professors who are inclined to resist multiculturalism in the first place may complain about students' not being prepared for college work, irrespective of the actual ability and intelligence of these students.

In a committee meeting involving a faculty advisory committee, some faculty members were complaining about the general writing ability of ethnic minority students on campus. One of us (JSM) tried to normalize it by pointing out that when he was at Washington State University, a campus that was 95% White, he was astonished at the horrible level of writing ability of those students. This opened the door for some other faculty members who had been at other campuses to affirm that there were similarly low levels of writing ability across settings and ethnicities. Again, however, if someone wants to resist the ideals of multiculturalism, there are ample ways of framing the issue in socially acceptable, covertly racist manners (unintentional or otherwise).

Stereotyping

Related to complaints about "less prepared" students, but less covert a manner of resisting, is the stereotyping of ethnic minority students in ways that serve to support resistance. For example, Asian students represent the largest ethnic minority group on our campus (40% of all students). The stereotype of these Asian students as being good in mathematics is a subtle way of saying that they are not good in other subjects. As Sue and Abe (1988) pointed out, Asian students whose English is their second language quite often choose to take more mathematics courses because language is less of an issue in these courses. Thus, taking a lot of mathematics courses may not be an issue of ability, it may be an issue of survival.

This stereotype can be taken too far, as well. As was mentioned at the beginning of Chapter 4, a Vietnamese refugee told one of us (JSM) that his mathematics professor accused him of not trying very hard in the class. This student was receiving a C but the professor expected him to be receiving an A despite the fact that he had come from a poor rural village in Vietnam and had not had much schooling before his family had had to flee the country. Thus, he did not feel that he had any inherent ability in mathematics, yet he was feeling extra pressure because of his professor's stereotype of him.

Another Asian student said that she could not get into an architecture course because the professor told her that Asian students never do well in architecture and end up dropping out, anyway. Thus, she would be taking the space from another student who had a better chance of success in the course. This is a curious comment, given that three of this professor's colleagues in the School of Architecture were Asian, so this professor's assumption about the genetic endowment of architecture ability was disproven by his own collegial interaction. By the way, one of the Asian architecture professors is a very good professor and is very popular on campus. Perhaps if the stereotyping professor had never been exposed to this Asian professor, it would be a different story, but the Asian colleague is a widely recognized, active, outgoing professor who would be hard to overlook.

Stereotyping is not limited to ethnicity. As mentioned in Chapter 4, a mathematics professor at Washington State University felt that women did not have the mental discipline to be good at mathematics. However, the president of Vladivostok University felt that women could not excel in anything *but* subjects like mathematics, medicine, and the sciences. Obviously, sexism is not limited to the United States.

Small Numbers of Committed Faculty

As indicated in the Slow to Change section, despite the number of opportunities on campus for greater exposure to multicultural issues, very few faculty members actually take advantage of these opportunities. Because of the small number of these faculty members, there are precious few allies to help spread the word about multiculturalism. Moreover, resistant professors can reason, "Our department is addressing multiculturalism. So-and-so is representing our department on this issue."

☐ Staff

The staff members, too, tend to change slowly, although they change more quickly than the faculty, at least partly because of the relatively high turnover rate among staff (at least, in comparison with the faculty turnover rate), and the requirement that those who replace departed staff must fulfill the more stringent criterion of sensitivity to multicultural issues. Also, the staff tends to work in a hierarchical structure, so directives from the top filter down through the staff at a much more rapid pace and are taken more seriously. Although the faculty has a hierarchical structure as well, the system governing them tends to be much more egalitarian, and checks and balances equalize their positions to a much greater extent than occurs among the staff.

Finally, the staff at this university is much more diverse than the faculty, so multiculturalism touches their lives more directly than it does faculty lives.

Across this campus, the staff members tend to hold a much more positive view of multiculturalism than do the faculty. Certainly, when opportunities for training about multiculturalism arise, we have observed many more staff members attending than faculty members. Moreover, on this campus, many staff members volunteer to become involved with the organization and planning of diversity workshops and conferences, participate in cultural organizations such as the Latino/a Faculty, Staff, and Student Association, and serve as advisors to ethnic student organizations (every student organization must have a faculty or staff mem-ber to serve as an official advisor who approves the activities of the organizations).

For the past 3 years, one of us (JSM) has been a member of the planning committee for the annual Cross-Cultural Retreat held at a site off campus (see Chapter 7 for a discussion of this activity). The organizers have put out a general call for people to help with the organization of the retreat. In my 3 years on this committee, I (JSM) have been the only professor who has been involved with the planning (one year, another professor volunteered to be on the committee, but she attended only two meetings and did not even attend the retreat). Organizers have typically been staff members and a few student volunteers. At the retreat itself, the overwhelming number of participants are students, with many staff members being small-group facilitators as well as participants. Typically, only 5 to 10 of the 170 to 200 participants attending this retreat are professors, and most of those who do attend do so every year.

☐ Students

Students here on campus exhibit the most diverse response to multiculturalism among all of the subsets of the university environment. Certainly, the diversity of the student body itself contributes to the diversity of response to this issue. Some push for more multicultural opportunities, others oppose such initiatives, many ignore them, and some just tolerate them. Quite often, students merely mirror the attitudes of their favorite faculty members. Because of the power differential, they may reflect these attitudes to gain the favor of these faculty members, or they may be truly convinced of the attitudes because of their connection with these instructors. As Erikson (1968) indicated, individuals at this life stage (at least those who enter college right after high school graduation) may be forming or firming their identities, and influential others may have profound effects upon this identity formation.

A number of students are the first in their families to attend college and are from ethnic groups that have vested interests in the acceptance of multiculturalism by the campus community. We have, for example, a large Latino student population (25%), many of whom have strong national identities and have demanded services, programs, and activities that specifically address their unique needs. Problems sometimes occur, however, when the attention of these groups is exclusively focused on themselves. If the Latino community is not trying to establish an inclusive environment for Asian American and African American and Native American students as well, then tension between groups may arise.

☐ Conclusions

Although there is a strong push for diversity and multiculturalism at the top levels of this university, resistance to this push may come from many levels and in many forms. Perhaps the primary source of resistance is the faculty, as the faculty have various means of counterbalancing the power of the president and other administrators. These resistances were discussed in Chapter 3, but one form of resistance not discussed earlier is simply a fundamental resistance to change. In this case, faculty may not necessarily be resistant or subtly racist, they may simply resist attempts to add material to their curricula. For one thing, such additions may necessarily have to replace topics faculty members hold near and dear to their hearts. Such additions also require them to retool and understand other domains before they can comfortably include them in the courses they teach. Because of their own resistance, they may have a profound effect upon students who may desire to reflect the values and attitudes of these professors. The principal solution to this form of resistance is for the administration to offer a number of rewards for the inclusion of multiculturalism into curricula or personal growth and to make judicious use of pressures that encourage all those on campus to aim for the goal of multiculturalism.

☐ References

Cox, T., Jr. (1994). *Cultural diversity in organizations: Theory, research and practice.* San Francisco: Berrett-Koehler.

Erikson, E. H. (1968). *Identity: Youth and crisis.* New York: Norton.

McIntosh, P. (1986, April). *White privilege and male privilege: A personal account of coming to see correspondences through work in women's studies.* Paper presented at the Virginia Women's Studies Association Conference, Richmond, VA.

Sue, S., & Abe, J. (1988). *Predictors of academic achievement among Asian American and White students* (College Board Report No. 88-11). New York: College Entrance Examination Board.

Sue, S., & Zane, N. (1987). The role of culture and cultural techniques in psychotherapy: A critique and reformulation. *American Psychologist, 42,* 37–45.

9
CHAPTER

Addressing Resistance
at the Administrative Level

In 1991, when President Suzuki took office at California State Polytechnic University, Pomona (known as Cal Poly Pomona for short), he had two major initiatives on his agenda: improved technology for the campus and an appreciation for multiculturalism. His efforts fit into a broader, system-wide and societal context that supported these two initiatives. His multicultural initiative, however, was not the beginning of the multicultural effort on campus. This chapter discusses the many administrative efforts that have been undertaken to not only diversify the campus community but also to help individuals appreciate multiculturalism, both here and in society at large. These efforts are particular to this campus, but we believe they may be adapted to other campuses that have similarly committed administrators.

As discussed in Chapter 6, creating a multicultural campus community requires a great deal of patience and a firm resolve on the part of administrators if it is to have any chance of succeeding. It is easy to put the issue aside whenever other matters appear on the agenda of the president's cabinet. A stated commitment by senior administrators along with documents affirming and delineating that commitment do not guarantee that a cultural change will be accomplished. It is important, indeed imperative, that the agreed-upon commitments be implemented and assessed. Markers must be in place to ensure that progress is being made toward the desired outcome.

Additionally, the programs and activities described later should not be viewed as discrete entities but rather as interrelated pieces of a larger mosaic of efforts all pointed toward the common goal—creation of a diverse community.

Finally, it is important to note that even more effective than support from the administration is the substantial impact of grassroots efforts. Many of the programs we discuss here were started by individuals who banded together, coalescing around issues of pressing concern to them. Administrative support often followed, but it was the faculty, staff, and students who provided the initial impetus and the sustained effort that led to the success of the various programs and initiatives.

☐ Cross-Cultural Retreat

The current president's tenure began in 1991, but efforts to change the campus environment toward the appreciation of diversity had started at least several years before his arrival. The university was predominantly White before the president's tenure began, but a small group of ethnic minority and White majority staff and students had pushed to establish an annual event called the Cross-Cultural Retreat. This retreat began on the Martin Luther King, Jr., weekend in 1988 and has been held annually every year since. It began with 20 or 30 individuals who held the retreat to affirm their commitment to multicultural issues and to strategize about how to improve the campus climate.

Over the years, the Cross-Cultural Retreat has grown to include nearly 200 participants. As discussed in Chapter 7, it is primarily student-based, with staff next in number, and with faculty contributing just a few participants. The retreat has become so popular that in recent years, because of space limitations, it has had to turn away individuals who have wanted to attend. It has now become institutionalized to the extent that those who desire to be in positions of leadership (for example, people desiring to become residential advisors in student housing) and will be working with our diverse student population are required to attend the event.

The retreat addresses issues involving a broad range of types of diversity, including racial and ethnic diversity, gender, sexual orientation, religious diversity, and socioeconomic class differences. These issues are addressed on a rotating basis, with each retreat dealing with one to four topics. The goals of the retreat are to raise awareness of these issues in participants' minds and to begin to teach the skills needed to respond to situations involving such topics. Moreover, participants are given packets of information about other events on campus that address these issues. Finally, there is a reunion several weeks after the retreat that celebrates diversity, helps to maintain the enthusiasm generated by the weekend, reminds participants of upcoming multicultural programs, and allow people to share memories of the event.

Because of the large number of participants each year, and to try to ensure that sensitive topics can be handled appropriately and that all participants can share their thoughts and feelings, small group sessions have been incorporated into the retreat. Many who have attended retreats previously return to facilitate small groups. In large group exercises, quite often there are sessions that encourage group discussion, but because of the large number of participants, only a relatively small number of people are able to voice their opinions or feelings. In contrast, the small group sessions (consisting of 7 to 12 individuals, including two facilitators) offer participants an opportunity to express themselves, delve more deeply into issues, and understand how to apply the exercises to their everyday lives. The facilitators have their own experience as previous attendees from which to draw, and they are required to attend two additional training sessions before the retreat. One of these sessions addresses general issues of group facilitation, and the other allows the facilitators to experience some of the exercises to be used in the retreat and to understand the arrangement of the schedule for the entire weekend.

The small group facilitators also meet during meals and break periods to discuss any problems or concerns that arise in discussion groups. In many respects, the small group facilitators are the backbone of the Cross-Cultural Retreat weekend, as they are in closest contact with the participants throughout the retreat and therefore can have the greatest impact on those individuals.

The Cross-Cultural Retreat is the primary responsibility of a staff member of the Office of Student Life. Also, the advisors of the cultural centers (to be discussed in the next section) are required to be on the planning committee for the retreat weekend. Former participants and other interested individuals volunteer to be on the committee as well, bringing the total to about 12 members. Each is assigned or volunteers for a subcommittee task, such as planning the program, securing donations from local merchants, planning the reunion, or designing, collecting, and analyzing evaluations of the retreat.

In general, participants find the Cross-Cultural Retreat to be a very valuable experience. Interestingly, the two most common suggestions for improvement are the contradictory requests for more free time to interact with other participants and for more structured time to discuss the exercises with the whole group. We say that these are contradictory because both require large blocks of time, yet participants would like the overall time commitment at the retreat to remain about the same because the intensity of the experience causes them to be emotionally drained by the end of the weekend.

As a side note, the most enjoyable time for JSM is the annual talent show that is held on the Saturday night of the retreat. Here, participants sing, dance, play the guitar, perform skits, or recite poems they have written or that have been written by well-known poets. At his first retreat, JSM was so impressed with the talent on the campus that it immediately made him feel much more connected with and proud of the university.

☐ Cultural Centers

To retain underrepresented students and because of the desire of groups for a comfortable place to meet, interact, and receive advice, a building at the heart of the campus was remodeled to create a space for them. This signaled the birth of the cultural centers. In the beginning, 4 years ago, three centers existed—the Chicano/Latino Center (now the Cesar E. Chavez Center), the Asian Pacific Islander Center, and the African American Center. A year later, as the administration attempted to address the needs of the gay/lesbian/bisexual/transsexual students, the Pride Center opened its doors. The remodeled building also houses The CENTER, a facility that provides services to women and reentry students. Eventually, thanks largely to the efforts of a volunteer outreach team composed of faculty, staff, and students, a number of American Indian students were recruited to the campus, and a place was provided for them in a space vacated by the Pride Center. The Pride Center's move to another building allowed for greater privacy and helped to preserve the confidentiality of students who wished to keep their orientations a private matter while still allowing them the ability to secure services from the Pride Center.

Advisors to the centers play key roles in helping students achieve their educational goals by advising them about classes, setting up tutorial sessions, and counseling them on personal problems. They are also required to plan and implement a history month and other important events related to their group's affiliation (an African American/Black History Month, an Asian/Pacific Islander History Month, a Gay, Lesbian, Bisexual, and Transsexual History Month, and so forth).

It is worth noting that the cultural centers model we developed allows for autonomously functioning centers that are housed in the same building. This was done to ensure that each underrepresented group had a separate, distinct space they could call their own. The potential drawback to this occurs if a group chooses to isolate itself from the other centers and the rest of the campus. What has actually occurred was not totally predictable. When the centers were established, despite each group's adamant desire to keep their activities confined to their group only, gradually, the centers have engaged in more and more joint programming. We believe this growing cohesion as a multicultural student community is a result of the developmental phase in which these students now find themselves. Had we tried to force the groups to work together 4 years ago, we probably would not have succeeded. Each of the groups separately had to first establish a sense of comfort and a place within the university before its members could venture forth and work with other groups. In the years ahead, our expectation is that the groups will engage more frequently in mainstream activities such as student government and fraternities and sororities. This appears to be the next phase in their eventual full integration into campus life.

☐ The Unity Luncheon

Years ago, the various ethnic specific-faculty, staff, and student associations held separate annual luncheons at the beginning of each academic year. When President Suzuki arrived at Cal Poly Pomona, these groups decided to get together and implement an annual Unity Luncheon to celebrate diversity on campus. This event draws 130 to 200 people from across campus at the beginning of each year for lunch, culturally oriented entertainment, and a keynote speaker who addresses issues of diversity. The associations take turns assuming the lead in the planning of the luncheon, and the other associations provide representatives to help with the event.

About 4 years ago, the Gay/Lesbian/Bisexual/Transsexual Faculty, Staff, and Student Association (GLBTFSSA) asked to participate in the planning of the luncheon, as they had strongly supported the event over the years. Many members of the ethnically specific groups did not want GLBTFSSA's inclusion and changed the name of the luncheon to the Unity of Colors Luncheon in order to prevent the GLBTFSSA from participating. As one might imagine, this caused a great deal of strife not only between the GLBTFSSA and the ethnically specific groups but also within the ethnic associations themselves. Many individuals on campus openly boycotted the Unity Luncheon because of the exclusion of the GLBTFSSA, and many members of the ethnically specific groups refused to work on the committee because of the exclusion.

When the rotation of the luncheon's leadership fell upon the shoulders of the Asian/Pacific Faculty, Staff, and Student Association (APFSSA) 3 years ago, one of us (JSM) was president of the APFSSA and insisted upon the inclusion of the GLBTFSSA in the luncheon's planning. By that time, many on the planning committee who had initially been opposed to their inclusion had come to know members of the GLBTFSSA through other committees and activities and had grown to better understand their lifestyle choices. Moreover, they valued the contributions these members had made to the other committees. Thus, they were open to the GLBTFSSA's involvement. As one member stated with a smile, "My understanding has evolved over the years." Another member of the planning committee, however, was still quite opposed to this restructuring. But the Vice President for Student Affairs and a financial supporter of the event (and coauthor of this book—GIA) addressed the committee and strongly supported the inclusion of the GLBTFSSA as a full partner in the planning process. When the one member opposed to inclusion voiced her opinion, the vice president indicated that if the association were not accepted, his office would withdraw its financial support. Although still opposed to the inclusion, the member finally acquiesced.

Thus, the GLBTFSSA has been institutionalized as a full partner in the planning of the luncheon, and the name has been changed back to the Unity Luncheon. Clearly, the threat of withdrawal of resource support is not the preferred way to achieve the full participation and inclusion of all groups in a unity celebration, but when no other option is available to deal with stubborn prejudices, firm action must be taken to achieve the desired goal. In the situation described above, every effort was made to present the case of the need for the cultural groups to demonstrate and model a philosophy of inclusion. However, when this approach failed, strong action was needed.

☐ The University Diversity Committee

In 1993, President Suzuki appointed a University Diversity Committee to examine the campus climate around issues of diversity and to develop and implement a plan that included efforts to impact hiring practices, admissions, academic programs, and special-interest organizations. Among the recommendations contained in the report was one that urged institution of a Faculty Diversity Program, in which half of the salary of an ethnic minority hired by an academic department would be assumed by the university for the first year. Thus, it was a fiscal advantage for a department to hire a new ethnic minority faculty member. Once on campus, the ethnic minority faculty member was eligible to apply for a teaching load reduction under the auspices of the Affirmative Action Faculty Development Program. This program was designed to reduce the teaching load of these faculty members during the first year so that they could work on research or other activities that would enhance their chances for tenure. If granted, the faculty members were released from one course each quarter, which on our campus is a one-third reduction in teaching load for an academic term.

Other recommendations by the University Diversity Committee that were implemented were the Affirmative Action Professional and Staff Development Grant, the Pilot Executive Leadership and Development Program, the Task Force on Sexual/Gender Harassment, and the Reaffirming Ethnic Awareness and Community Harmony (REACH) Program.

The Affirmative Action Professional and Staff Development Grant was established to assist new ethnic minority staff members to address any professional development concerns or needs they may have.

The Pilot Executive Leadership and Development Program was designed to identify promising ethnic minority and female faculty members and train them for college administrative positions. These individuals were provided with funding so they could attend various leadership conferences, which would make them more likely to succeed when applying for college administrative positions later in their careers.

The Task Force on Sexual/Gender Harassment examined the campus climate on such issues. The sexual/gender harassment policy was rewritten by the task force to clarify and affirm zero tolerance for violations. This new policy has been widely acclaimed by groups supporting women's rights on campus.

REACH, first developed by GIA at University of California, Irvine, is a diversity training program for students in a class format. These students take courses in multicultural awareness, receive training in the skills of dealing with interracial conflict, general conflict resolution, and the like. Upon completion of the program, the students are expected to become involved in campus activities concerned with issues of diversity, such as the Cross-Cultural Retreat, special symposia on multiculturalism, and working with invited speakers who address multicultural concerns. The students also conduct diversity training programs in residence halls, student organizations, and academic classes. Students are recruited from the Greek community, student government, clubs, and organizations as well as from the ethnic-specific student associations. The goal is to develop among these key student stakeholders and leaders an appreciation for and an understanding of working together to achieve community harmony.

☐ The Unity Through Diversity Initiative

President Suzuki also initiated a program called the Unity through Diversity Initiative. The initiative provided training for faculty, staff, and students about multicultural issues, such as the series of multicultural programs presented in the spring of 1995, the fall of 1995, and the spring of 1996. He also offered a two-day charette on diversity in the spring of 1998, in which faculty, staff, and students were presented with programs on diversity and were also able to share their thoughts, feelings, and resistances about concerns related to diversity. The format was similar to that of the Cross-Cultural Retreat, but it was held on campus during business hours.

☐ Special Assistant for Affirmative Action and Diversity

To oversee diversity programs on campus and to be the president's eyes and ears at programs he could not attend (President Suzuki regularly attends many programs himself, even if only as a welcoming speaker), President Suzuki hired a Special Assistant for Affirmative Action and Diversity. The Special Assistant participated in the Cross-Cultural Retreat and other such programs. In addition, she helped to implement the recommendations of the University Diversity Committee. Along with overseeing faculty and staff hiring to ensure that affirmative action procedures were being followed, the special assistant was responsible for overseeing the university's involvement in a number of programs. These programs included the California State University Forgivable Loan/Doctoral Incentive Program for Minorities and Women, the Presidents' Commission on Enhancing the Campus Environment for Women and Minorities, and the diversity programs mentioned above.

☐ Faculty Center for Professional Development

One of the most highly respected offices on campus is the Faculty Center for Professional Development. The office is staffed by a director, a secretary, and an advisory committee composed of one faculty member from each college and school on campus. As the duties and obligations of the office began to expand, the president responded to the office's needs by hiring another support staff member and three faculty associates. The associates' charge is to provide input and expertise in the areas of instructional technology, student outcomes assessment, and diversity. Significantly for the university, the issue of diversity received equal weighting with the other areas of faculty support. The diversity associate's job is to help coordinate campus activities in diversity, making sure that faculty are informed about the programs on campus and are encouraged to attend.

☐ Post-Proposition 209 Efforts

Most, if not all, of the above activities generated and encouraged by the Office of the President were conducted in the pre-Proposition 209 environment. As discussed in Chapter 3, Proposition 209, which was passed by California voters, eliminated affirmative action programs as then defined and implemented, so a radical reexamination of existing programs had to be conducted on campus.

First, President Suzuki, who had publicly stated his opposition to Proposition 209 at his President's Convocation in the fall of 1996, formed a committee to recommend a university-wide plan to ensure that the spirit of diversity was maintained in our institutional programs, while complying with the new law. This committee was made up of 27 people from the campus, including members from Administrative Affairs, Student Affairs, and Academic Affairs and one from each of the eight colleges and schools. These individuals were sent to a conference in Florida called Educating One-third of a Nation, VI: Diversity, Opportunity and American Achievement. The committee brought back successful models to deal with diversity issues. Moreover, it was hoped that the representatives would reenergize their colleagues in their support of the commitment to diversity goals.

The Racial Legacies Forum

One recent effort was the campus' participation in a teleconference sponsored by the White House called "Racial Legacies and Learning: An American Dialogue." The goal was to have community leaders join with institutional stakeholders to dialogue about the issue of race relations. As part of this teleconference, participants viewed a documentary film, "Skin Deep," that examined race relations on a college campus through interviews, following students through their campus lives and at home and focusing on a weekend retreat dealing with race relations in which the students had participated. In their own accounts, the students reported that they had been transformed by the experience, which gave the audience a sense of the possibility of change in this domain.

After viewing the film, teleconference participants were able to engage in a dialogue with one another across the country. Following the dialogue, breakout groups were formed, issues were discussed, and recommendations were made for strategies that would facilitate racial harmony on campus. These recommendations fell into seven categories: workshops, curriculum, faculty, students, research, Cal Poly Pomona and the internal community, and Cal Poly Pomona and the external community. The box summarizes the recommendations that came out of the workshop, as compiled by Dr. Vinita Dhingra, who was the lead person at Cal Poly Pomona for this project.

There was a Racial Legacies follow-up session that was held 5 months later at the following academic year's Fall Conference. Here, key individuals involved with the original Racial Legacies Forum provided information about the implementation of many of the ideas that had been suggested in the break-out sessions half a year earlier. As is apparent, there are many opportunities on campus for a person to become involved in the area of multiculturalism. It should be mentioned, however, that attendees at these important diversity events are usually the same ones who attend every event.

As we said in Chapter 6, questions remain about whether we are simply reinventing the wheel or truly developing valuable new programs that can help the university to create a model community for the next millennium.

Leadership Development Program for Higher Education

Noticing the dearth of Asian/Pacific Americans in university leadership positions across the country—especially in relation to the high numbers of Asians receiving their doctorates—President Suzuki negotiated with a private, nonprofit organization to offer an annual training program, held on campus, to help Asian/Pacific Americans develop the skills necessary to attain leadership positions in higher education. The organization is the Los Angeles-based group Leadership Education for Asian Pacifics (LEAP). Beginning in 1997, the first class of 28

Category	Recommendations
	Summary and Recommendations from Breakout Discussions at the Racial Legacies Dialogue
Workshops	Continue to have workshops like the Racial Legacies Forum
	Bring students and community mentors to a Racial Legacies Forum
	Require workshops for all faculty, staff, and students
	Workshops should be more intensive (longer), and include follow-up
	Obtain "Skin Deep" and distribute it to the wider community
Curriculum	Integrate multiculturalism throughout the university curriculum
	Institutionalize throughout the curriculum (multitiered, minor)
	Don't limit this teaching to only Ethnic and Women Studies Department
	Restructure General Electives to include diversity
	Don't focus only on diversity content: include pedagogy
	Increase collaborative learning to bring diverse students together
	Don't use a standard lecture format
	Establish a multicultural component for the Teacher Education Program
	Make it mandatory in the grammar school curriculum
Faculty	Diversify faculty
	Educate and engage faculty to understand and value diversity
	Devise a faculty reward system for knowledge in this area
Students	Involve students in the planning, assessing, and research on diversity
	Require service learning for graduation; require seminar presentations
	Acknowledge that students are the bridge between the university and the community
	Provide volunteer opportunities in the community for students

(Continues on next page)

*Summary and Recommendations from Breakout Discussions
at the Racial Legacies Dialogue (Continued)*

Category	Recommendations
	Provide immersion in diversity issues for students
	Have upper-division students act as mentors to high school students
	Modify student evaluation forms to permit input on racial climate
	Have the Department of Institutional Research make this a priority
	What has the university already tried to do, and what are the outcomes of those efforts?
Research	Find corporate sponsors to fund faculty research efforts in this area
	Provide seed grants for faculty and students to study elements of Racial Legacy and values to diversity
	Reward and recognize contributions to diversity by faculty and staff
	Make icons of diversity more prominent on campus, e.g., murals
	Increase opportunities to connect with I-Poly (the International High School located on campus) and with the Children's Center
	Review admissions standards; evaluate for bias and seek ways to value diversity
	Ensure diversity in search committees
	Establish a Center of Cultural Information
	Establish a group for organizing creative opportunities to get people together
Cal Poly Pomona and the Internal Community	Create cross-community contact opportunities
	Make conscious efforts to develop resources— grants for students and faculty to collaborate
	Make it the university's mission, and do it now
	Get all administrators to make diversity a top priority and part of all their presentations; administrators should provide resources for this effort
	Stop preaching to the choir
	Align what we say with what we do

Summary and Recommendations from Breakout Discussions
at the Racial Legacies Dialogue (Continued)

Category	Recommendations
Cal Poly Pomona and the External Community	Engage the surrounding community in the dialogue, including those who won't eventually come to the university
	"Adopt a school" from surrounding community, provide workshops
	Reach out to Pomona and other surrounding communities
	Partnering with surrounding community is key to solution
	Partner with churches, business, chambers of commerce, law enforcement, as well as schools
	Involve alumni
	Invite parents to campus to share academic culture
	Celebrate diversity events (Black History Month, Hispanic Heritage Month, etc.) with community
	Bring minority kids to campus; make education *real*
	Provide free education; education brings different perspectives
	Work to overturn unfair legislation

Asian/Pacifics from across the country came to Cal Poly Pomona for an intensive 3½-day session on leadership. Topics included how an individual's adherence to Asian/Pacific values can help and hinder his or her chance of being selected for higher-level administrative positions, a review of the management styles of the participants, how to develop the skills necessary to improve opportunities for success, and how to learn effective communications styles. At this writing, several alumni of the training sessions have competed for and secured higher-level faculty and administrative positions. They have credited their success in part to what they learned at the Leadership Development Program for Higher Education.

The Women's Council of the State Universities

President Suzuki has been extremely supportive of the Women's Council of the State Universities (WCSU) programs, both on campus and statewide.

The campus has a very active WCSU chapter and the leader is a highly committed woman, Pat Davis (see below), who is among the most active individuals we know in the area of racial harmony, intercultural dialogue, diversity, and community. Every one of her WCSU programs combines women's issues with issues of diversity.

The CENTER

The CENTER includes "Women's Resources and ReEntry Services." The director, Pat Davis, is the woman to whom we were referring in relation to the WCSU. She has initiated numerous programs on campus, such as the Powerful Non-Defensive Communication Training workshop, a weekend retreat with Lillian Roybal Rose (a leading multicultural trainer), a Mediation/Conflict Resolution Program, a Women and Race Dialogue Group, a Men's Discussion Group, and a Men Against Violence Against Women campaign. She also sponsors the Students T.A.L.K. (Teaching Awareness Learning Knowledge) program that helps students understand issues of diversity. In addition, she plans and implements the Women's History Month events on campus every March. All of her programs have a heavy multicultural/diversity component to them. She is clearly one of the most valuable resources for information on this topic on campus.

Executive Director of Diversity and Compliance Programs

The President's Special Assistant for Affirmative Action and Diversity left for another position in 1996, and it is unclear whether her position, as structured, would have withstood the legal constrictions of Proposition 209. Because the university was still accepting federal support, and all agencies accepting such funds have to comply with federal regulations regarding affirmative action, and because we wanted to continue our work to create a more inclusive campus community, a new office was formed—the Office of Diversity and Compliance Programs. As a result of a national search, Dr. Donna Albro was hired in the spring of 1998 to serve as the university's new Director of Diversity and Compliance Programs. She has come to campus with a wealth of experience and enthusiasm for this area, and her office has been helpful in funding various projects. As an example, funding for the Cross-Cultural Retreat has always been problematic, and the previous year's planners had to hold the retreat duirng a Saturday and Sunday instead of the customary Friday, Saturday, and Sunday because of a shortage of funds. Dr. Albro said that she would fund the second night stayover if more faculty members could be recruited to attend. Although the number of faculty members who actually attended the conference was still disappointingly low, enough were present, and her office funded the second night.

Dr. Albro's office also funded a series on nondefensive communication, which was referred to in the previous section. Moreover, she purchased "The Way Home," a videotape that was designed to be the female equivalent of the popular videotape, "Color of Fear," which documents a weekend of ethnic minority and White men exploring issues of multiculturalism. During Women's History Month, there was a showing of "The Way Home," and Dr. Albro provided funding so that a few of the women in the film could come to campus to discuss the documentary.

Finally, Dr. Albro's office has provided support to a number of faculty and staff members so they could attend the annual Summer Institute for Intercultural Communication that takes place in Oregon. This is a well-known training institute that is held over a 3-week period. Clearly, Dr. Albro has been a great addition to the campus community, and those of us involved with multicultural work are quite pleased with her contributions to the diversity efforts.

A Culture-Focused Academic Program

Finally, in an effort to broaden and deepen the entire campus community's understanding of the various cultural experiences that are represented here at Cal Poly Pomona and in the larger world, quarter-long, multifaceted programs are periodically offered at Cal Poly Pomona. They are created with significant academic content, focusing on a particular country or culture through special class offerings, notable speakers, and music, dance, and theater performances. The most recent was The Zimbabwe Quarter, which included visits and lectures from Zimbabwe dignitaries and a performance by the internationally acclaimed dance and music company Black Umfolosi. Other culturally focused quarters have included the Asian Heritage Quarter. The College of Letters, Arts, and Social Sciences initiated the program and has always provided significant support and resources for the culture-oriented activities. Other significant contributors over the years have included the Office of the President, the Division of Academic Affairs, the International Center, the College of the Extended University, and various academic departments in several other schools and colleges.

☐ Conclusions

As may be seen from the discussion, under the administration's leadership and with the assistance of many committed members of the faculty, staff, and student body, the university has been able to offer a wide array of programs and activities to make the campus a more inclusive place. Unfortunately, we have been unable to establish broad-based involvement and often find ourselves "preaching to the choir" (see Chapter 10).

We cannot offer any definitive solutions to this problem. However, we are hopeful, because the circle of those involved in diversity activities on our campus, though still small, has expanded and is continuing to grow. Our recommendation to administrators is that they demonstrate a firm, ongoing commitment to advancing the cause of multiculturalism. And if the administrators try to ensure that the needs of those campus community members who may still be skeptical about the virtue and value of embracing diversity are considered as well, they will have gone a long way toward establishing the trust and support—the earned credibility—needed to achieve their goal.

Gradually, if administrators stay the course, it is our expectation that the cynics who want to wait out the administration or who might feel marginalized by the administration's diversity program will find fewer and fewer people willing to listen to their negative rhetoric. Despite the strong resistance we have encountered over the years, programs can succeed and have succeeded here. This is an excellent indication that the programs and initiatives we've discussed have a good chance of succeeding on campuses across the country as well as in settings in which people are ready to transform themselves into a model community for the 21st century.

Where Do We Go from Here?

As many know, although opportunities for experience in the multicultural domain are many, participation is limited. A major and vexing problem remains: how can we get beyond preaching to the choir and start attracting those who are less sensitive and less open so they will participate in multicultural programs and gain an appreciation for the importance of this issue? Racism remains strong in this country, and most people do not really understand how they are contributing to this problem. Eliminating racism is perhaps the most important work we can do. Certainly, the horrific bloody massacres in Rwanda, Bosnia-Herzegovina, and Kosovo underscore how ethnic strife can spin out of control if left unattended. Going beyond the preaching of sermons to the choir is one way of helping to eliminate racism.

Although I see going beyond the choir as the most important next step, it is clearly not the only future step in multiculturalism. Many in the multicultural movement remain reluctant to support other causes, such as feminism, lesbian and gay issues, and issues of disability. However, we are all in this fight together, and those who support multiculturalism must understand the importance of building alliances with those struggling with the same issues but from different perspectives.

☐ Going Beyond Preaching to the Choir

In the particular sense, the issue of getting beyond preaching to the choir will solve itself. Most professional organizations recognize the

163

importance of multiculturism because of the changing demographics of the United States. As McCombs (1998) indicated, by the middle of the next century, ethnic minorities will constitute approximately 50% of the population of the United States, so professional organizations are now beginning to realize their professional responsibility to train future professionals in multiculturalism. If they do not, they would be doing a disservice to the very constituents they claim to prepare and support. Therefore, eventually most of the leaders of tomorrow will have been exposed to multiculturalism and know its importance. Because of this near inevitability, should we just wait for its evolution, or should we work to hasten its arrival? Of course we should work toward its arrival sooner rather than later.

One of the more influential speeches I have heard was given by Juan Williams. As most people know, Juan Williams is the Pulitzer Award winning author of *Eyes on the Prize*, a television documentary about the Civil Rights Movement (Hampton, 1986). Mr. Williams came to speak at Washington State University while I was a professor there. As I have mentioned before, Washington State is a predominantly White university. In fact, 95% of the student population is White. Mr. Williams rhetorically asked, "Why should White students care if ethnic minorities are on campus? Because you are the future leaders of America. America will be predominantly occupied by people of color sometime next century, and if you do not learn how to communicate with people of color now, how can you possibly expect to be a leader in the future?"

Another justification of the importance of understanding issues of diversity by those who might otherwise be resistant came from Laura Brown. Dr. Brown is a well-known psychologist from Seattle who ran for APA president in 1997. She was a participant in the first National Multicultural Conference and Summit in January 1999. In an interview, she was asked why being aware of issues of diversity was important. Her response was something like this: "You don't know if you or one of your children will become disabled in the future; you don't know if one of your children will fall in love with an ethnic minority individual or a gay or lesbian individual in the future. These are not uncommon events, so it is not out of the realm of possibility that one of these situations may happen to you. If something like this does happen to you, will you be prepared to handle it? If not, it could have a major impact upon your life and the lives of your children, and the damage may be irreparable. Thus, it would behoove you to get training in this area in the absence of a highly emotional context. Should one of these situations happen to you, you would be much better prepared to handle it. Should one of these situations not happen to you, you will, at worse, simply be a better person for having undergone the experience." (I later had the opportunity to check with Dr. Brown about this characterization, and she affirmed that she responded in words to this effect.)

My own efforts to address this issue of going beyond preaching to the choir have been to try to find areas that cut across interests. For example, here on campus, I have tried to participate in discussions involving classroom management in the current, multicultural environment. Professors who may be insensitive to issues of multiculturalism may at least be interested in learning skills that might make their lives a bit easier in the classroom. I was the campus discussant on a national teleconference concerned with overcoming violence in the classroom, and I was able to expose the participants to issues of multiculturalism while advising them on techniques for deescalating various situations. At APA conventions, I have tried to present topics that deal with the teaching of multicultural issues (e.g., Mio, 1996). My reasoning is that quite often, people who are not "choir members" are not interested in the issue of multiculturalism per se, but because they are academics, issues concerning the teaching of multiculturalism can be of interest to them. Whereas the actual conduct of culturally sensitive counseling can be an emotional experience, the teaching of this material is a bit more intellectual. Those who might otherwise be resistant to this area but who feel somewhat guilty about not knowing enough about it may find it psychologically easier to engage in an intellectual discussion about the matter. I might add that I recently gave a presentation on my reaction paper technique at the 1999 Lewis M. Terman Western Regional Teaching Conference (Mio, 1999), and the room was almost completely filled. One White male in particular was quite interested in my presentation because he had been assigned to teach his department's multicultural course the next term. Ever since that time, he has e-mailed me constantly in order to learn more about how to teach such a course, so it appears that my strategy of focusing on teaching may be successful.

☐ Feminism

In many respects, I find it difficult to believe that everyone is not supportive of issues related to feminism. As Roades (1999) indicates, "The most widely accepted current definition [of feminism] involves the belief in and action towards the social, political, and economic equality between the sexes." If one asks, "Do you think that everyone should be treated fairly?" I cannot imagine anyone's saying no. However, it is the case that there remains a great deal of resistance to issues involving feminism in this country. In my classes on diversity, I like to read a newspaper article about a woman from Salt Lake City, Utah, who tried to change the name on her driver's license back to her birth name after her divorce (Utah Driver's Long Fight, 1991). The Utah Drivers' License Bureau said that she would have to have permission from her former husband to make the change. After the gasps from my students, I read further. Not only did she lose her case in court, she also lost her case on appeal in the U.S. District Court. So not only are many individuals resistant to treating women fairly, it is actually written into law that women not be treated fairly.

Because Proposition 209 has been such a major issue here in California, and because California has been such a bellwether for the country, I again discuss it here. Not only were ethnic minorities specifically mentioned as being excluded from special consideration or affirmative action for state college admissions and state government contracts, women were specifically mentioned, as well. However, equality was not the goal of this initiative, or it would have explicitly stated that *no one* would receive special consideration for admissions or contracts. But the initiative intentionally did not want to exclude special consideration for children of alumni or for geographically diverse (that is, rural) individuals, the vast majority of whom, in both categories, are White. So even though it seems that the struggle for women's rights has advanced farther than the struggle for multiculturalism, we should not ignore the needs of women in pursuing the ideals of multiculturalism. I, personally, have found that women have been my most important allies in the struggle for multiculturalism, and it would be unconscionable if I did not also fight for feminist ideals. I am heartened to see that in recent years, feminist scholars have recognized the need to integrate multiculturalism and feminism (e.g., Landrine, 1995).

☐ Lesbian and Gay Issues

Gay men and lesbians have been among the most vigorous supporters of multiculturalism, along with feminists, so it is incumbent upon ethnic minorities to be reciprocally supportive of gay and lesbian issues. Issues concerning the oppression of any out-group should be of concern to all, but especially to those targeted for oppression as well, so it would seem to be a natural reaction of reciprocity. However, in my experience, this has been one of the more difficult issues for many ethnic minorities to understand, appreciate, and put into action. As I mentioned, on my own campus, there was a great deal of resistance to the inclusion of the Gay, Lesbian, Bisexual, Transsexual Faculty, Staff, and Student Association in the Unity Luncheon. How paradoxical is that?

Perhaps one of the reasons this issue is so difficult is that most ethnic minority populations have a strong religious core around which the community is organized. This is not to stereotype all religions as being intolerant of issues of homosexuality, but it is a fact that in this country, many religions strongly reject homosexuality and are actively involved politically to suppress gays and lesbians by legislation. At the National Multicultural Conference and Summit, there was a session entitled "Facilitating Difficult Dialogues on Race, Gender, and Sexual Orientation" (Bingham, 1999). By far, the most spirited dialogue on this panel occurred among a lesbian, a heterosexual male ally, and a heterosexual male who was very open about his deeply held religious beliefs that spoke against homosexuality. This dialogue clearly indicated the distance we have to travel. If we cannot acknowledge oppression of another group and speak out against such oppression, how can we expect others to heed our calls?

As the brutal murder by dragging of James Byrd, Jr., in Jasper, Texas, reminded us all that overt, intentional racism still exists, so too did the murder of Matthew Shepard in Laramie, Wyoming, remind us of extreme homophobia. According to the editors of *Time* (1999):

> Taking turns, they [Russell Henderson and Aaron McKinney] allegedly began pounding Shepard on the head with a .357 Magnum revolver. The pair then drove about a mile east of town and, on Snowy Mountain View Road, they dragged Shepard out of the car. "They tied him to a post," said police commander Dave O'Malley, and as he begged for his life, they "beat him and beat him." The back of his head bashed to the brain stem, his face cut, his limbs scorched with burn marks, Shepard hung spread-eagled on a rough-hewn deer fence through a night of near freezing temperatures, unconscious and losing more and more blood. On the evening of the next day, 18 hours after he was abandoned, two bicyclists saw him. At first, they thought they were looking at a scarecrow. He was taken, barely alive, to a hospital where he died. (p. 95)

This chilling and brutal murder sent shock waves throughout the country. I cannot recall any public official who even remotely condoned the act, and they wanted to speak out against it. In the estimation of the editors of *Time*, the reaction against this murder was an indication of the changing mores of society:

> Shepard's brutal murder came at a time when the U.S. is buzzing with a dissonant debate over sexual orientation. What seems like an irresistible force of cultural change is meeting an immovable object of political

resistance. There may be more openly gay men and women in American now than in any other country at any other time in history. As a consequence, even the anti-gay right has had to shift the tone of its message as more and more straight Americans become acquainted with friends and family who are homosexual. (p. 95)

Perhaps as society becomes more comfortable with homosexuality, ethnic minority individuals will become more comfortable with homosexuality, as well. However, we should be at the forefront of this acceptance, not following society's lead.

☐ Issues Concerning Disability

One of the more contentious issues I see on the horizon is the issue of disability and the extent to which individuals with any kinds of disabilities should be treated the same as others with disabilities, or whether each group should be treated differently from one another. I say "contentious" because it seems that there are intelligent arguments on both sides of the issue. With the passage of the Americans with Disabilities Act of 1990, all individuals with any disability were legally covered when they insisted on appropriate accommodations for access and on antidiscriminatory practices in all public settings. That set the stage for conceptualizing all persons with disabilities as being in the same category. But experientially, it seems that a person who needs wheelchair access to a building is quite different from someone who needs a sign language interpreter. I brought up this issue at a luncheon meeting of blind individuals, and the ensuing discussion was quite lively, with audience participants talking passionately on both sides of the issue.

A second contentious issue involves treating individuals with disabilities as a minority group. At this point, it is unclear to me what the purpose of this classification is, but I know that it is important to some members of the disabled community. There is a Committee on Disability Issues in Psychology (CDIP). This committee has made a formal request to the APA governance structure to classify persons with disabilities as a minority group. However, all the documentation for this request was from the 1980s, before the Americans with Disabilities Act was passed. Before I joined the Committee on Ethnic Minority Affairs (CEMA), there was a heated meeting between CDIP and CEMA, with CDIP requesting CEMA's support on this issue, and members of CEMA being against the proposal. Again, I am unclear on the reasoning behind this request for classification. I read all of the documentation in support of it as presented by CDIP, and because the references were to situations that existed before 1990, I did not understand the advantage people with disabilities would gain by being classified as a minority group. Moreover, if they were classified as a minority group, would that mean that a separate committee focused on disability issues would have to be dissolved?

From my own perspective, I believe that we all need to recognize our roles as allies of individuals belonging to demographic groups that we ourselves are not a part of. If individuals with disabilities were to be classified as minorities, it would cloud the distinction between them and me. I believe that I can be a much more forceful ally of individuals with disabilities if those whom we are lobbying clearly see the distinction between the two of us. It would not seem that I would be lobbying for persons with disabilities for my own personal gain as an able-bodied ethnic minority individual. However, I am open to persuasion, and time will tell what the outcome of this issue will be. Incidentally, CDIP decided to formally withdraw its request for minority status; at this point, I do not know if they will revisit this issue or if it was withdrawn from any future consideration.

☐ Epilogue

The issue of addressing and even overcoming resistance to multiculturalism is, indeed, timely. Along with my colleagues, I have tried to present methods I have found useful over the years when addressing this resistance. These attempts are not presented as exhaustive but as suggestive. I hope the reader will find them helpful; I know that I have found it helpful to communicate my thoughts in this book. Together, we can work toward the elimination of discrimination in all forms and embrace multiculturalism as the tie that binds us all.

☐ References

Bingham, R. P. (1999, January). *Facilitating difficult dialogues on race, gender, and sexual orientation*. Demonstration at the National Multicultural Conference and Summit, Newport Beach, CA.

Editors of *Time*. (1999). *Time annual: The year in review 1998*. New York: Time Books.

Hampton, H. (Producer). (1986). *Eyes on the prize*. Boston: WGBH.

Landrine, H. (1995). *Bringing cultural diversity to feminist psychology: Theory, research, and practice*. Washington, DC: American Psychological Association.

McCombs, H. G. (1998, August). Mental health services in a managed care environment: Why cultural competence should matter. In T. L. Strickland (Chair), *Is managed care in your future?* Symposium presented at the 106th annual convention of the American Psychological Association, San Francisco.

Mio, J. S. (1996, August). Individual resistances in the classroom: Strategies for intervention. In J. S. Mio (Chair), *Institutional and individual resistances to multicultural issues: Discussions and interventions.* Symposium presented at the 104th annual convention of the American Psychological Association, Toronto, Canada.

Mio, J. S. (1999, April). *Teaching about multicultural issues: Reaction papers and the process of becoming aware.* Invited address at the 5th Lewis M. Terman Western Regional Teachers' Conference, Irvine, CA.

Roades, L. A. (1999). Feminism. In J. S. Mio, J. T. Trimble, P. Arredondo, H. E. Cheatham, & D. Sue (Eds.), *Key words in multicultural interventions: A dictionary.* Westport, CT: Greenwood.

Utah driver's long fight for her name on a license. (1991, July 12). *New York Times,* p. B7.

INDEX